D1617357

EDMUND BURKE

MODERNITY AND POLITICAL THOUGHT

Series Editor: Morton Schoolman
State University of New York at Albany

This unique collection of orginal studies of the great figures in the history of political and social thought critically examines their contributions to our understanding of modernity, its constitution, and the promise and problems latent within it. These works are written by some of the finest theorists of our time for scholars and students of the social sciences and humanities.

EDMUND BURKE:
MODERNITY, POLITICS, AND AESTHETICS

STEPHEN K. WHITE

Modernity and Political Thought
VOLUME 5

SAGE Publications
International Educational and Professional Publisher
Thousand Oaks   London   New Delhi

For information address:

SAGE Publications, Inc.
2455 Teller Road
Thousand Oaks, California 91320

SAGE Publications Ltd.
6 Bonhill Street
London EC2A 4PU
United Kingdom

SAGE Publications India Pvt. Ltd.
M-32 Market
Greater Kailash I
New Delhi 110 048 India

Printed in the United States of America

Library of Congress Cataloging-in-Publication Data

White, Stephen K.
    Edmund Burke : modernity, politics, and aesthetics / Stephen K. White.
        p.   cm. — (Modernity and political thought ; 5)
    Includes bibliographical references and index.
    ISBN 0-8039-3668-0 (cloth.) — ISBN 0-8039-3669-9 (pb.)
        1. Burke, Edmund, 1729-1797—Contributions in political science.
    I. Title. II. Series: Modernity and political thought ; vol. 5.
    JC176.B83W48   1994
    941.07′3′092—dc20   94-8568
                                                          CIP

94 95 96 97 10 9 8 7 6 5 4 3 2 1

Sage Production Editor: Diana E. Axelsen

To my Father
S. George White, Jr.

Contents

Series Editor's Introduction

S tephen K. White's *Edmund Burke: Modernity, Politics, and Aesthetics* is the fifth volume to appear in the Sage Series **Modernity and Political Thought.** White's contribution follows the recent publication of the initial four volumes in the series during the spring of 1993: William Connolly's *The Augustinian Imperative: A Reflection on the Politics of Morality;* Richard Flathman's *Thomas Hobbes: Skepticism, Individuality and Chastened Politics;* Fred Dallmayr's *G.W.F. Hegel: Modernity and Politics;* and Michael Shapiro's *Reading "Adam Smith": Desire, History and Value.* In 1994 *Edmund Burke* will be joined by studies of Jean-Jacques Rousseau by Tracy Strong, Henry David Thoreau by Jane Bennett, and Ralph Waldo Emerson by George Kateb. In the near future the series will conclude with contributions on Hannah Arendt by Seyla Benhabib, Michel Foucault by Thomas Dumm, Friedrich Nietzsche by Benjamin Barber, and Sigmund Freud by Jean Elshtain. As those who are familiar with the previous works of these authors will expect, these studies adopt a variety of approaches and pose importantly different questions. As contributors to **Modernity and Political Thought,** however, their efforts also are commonly devoted to effecting critical examinations of the contributions that major figures in

the history of political thought have made to our understanding of modernity—its constitution, problems, promises, and dangers which are latent
within it.

   Stephen White's study of Edmund Burke is unique for its analysis of the
aesthetic dimensions of Burke's writings and for the understanding of his
thought that an exposition of an aesthetic language provides. White laid
the foundations for his interpretation of Burke in his earlier work in social
and political theory. In *The Recent Work of Jürgen Habermas,* White ex-
amined theoretical developments in Habermas's critical theory which have
occurred since the English publication in 1971 of *Knowledge and Human
Interests* (originally published in German in 1968).[1] A sympathetic exposition of Habermas's attempt to articulate a critical, rationalist reconstruc-
tion of the Enlightenment, White's study also accomplished the difficult
task of assessing Habermas's theory of communicative action from the
standpoint of its significance for social thought, the philosophy of the social sciences, and, perhaps most importantly from the perspective of the
study presently under consideration, for ethical theory and our understanding of modernity. It is in this latter area that White took up the most
problematic issues confronting Habermas's theoretical allegiance to uni-
versalist reason and ethics as well as the defense of modernity that his
universalism entails. Of special concern were those challenges to Habermas's thinking that emerged from the development of contextualist and
relativist positions on rationality—described by White as "a shift in philosophical consciousness"—during the period in which his theory of communicative action began to mature.

   White's exposition of Habermas's response to these serious challenges
indicates that he clearly shares Habermas's deep concern with whether
moral appeals can be accorded some sort of defensible universal status. In
his estimation, communicative rationality offers promise of sustaining the
universality of moral claims without thereby rendering them so hopelessly
abstract that their determinacy can be salvaged only by culturally concre-
tizing them and thus compromising their universal validity. White finds
equally attractive Habermas's strong association of universal validity claims
with the theoretical and practical competencies of members of modern
societies as an approach to constituting a defense of modernity and certain
crucial values of a modern culture. At the same time, White stresses that
the value of Habermas's theory does not lie simply in its philosophical

contributions, but as a vehicle for thinking about how modern societies already contain within them the means through which they may be reconstituted.

In brief, then, White underscores the contribution of the model of communicative reason and action, along with the contributions of its critics, to one of the decisive questions of contemporary philosophy, "what it means to create some legitimate commonality among different forms of life, 'legitimate' here carrying the sense of reciprocity and mutual respect?" Thus it is not merely the ethical matter of the grounds for the legitimacy of modernity to which Habermas speaks directly in White's study of the development of his work. But it is the "legitimacy," broadly speaking, of different and competing forms of political and social life with which White is here concerned.

This orientation informs White's own recent work, *Political Theory and Postmodernism,* where his primary intention is to illuminate ethical and political questions which surface in the contestations between postmodern and modernist social thought.[2] Once again, Habermas's theory of communicative action is an axis around which White constructs his argument, although on this occasion Habermas's critics are granted considerably more space. White begins this work by conceptualizing postmodernism in terms of a problematic constituted by four phenomena: a growing incredulity toward metanarratives, a new awareness of the costs of societal rationalization, the explosion of information technologies, and the emergence of new social movements. Rather than the problematic itself, what is interesting for our purposes is his particular approach to elucidating this problematic.

To this end he introduces two sets of distinctions. The first is between *a sense of responsibility to act* and *a sense of responsibility to otherness.* The former sense of responsibility refers to acting in the world in justifiable ways, to a moral-prudential obligation to acquire reliable knowledge, achieve practical ends in a defensible manner, solve problems, realize certain values, and meet the expectations of others. The latter—and opposing—sense of responsibility refers, however, to exposing and rejecting the devaluation and discipline of an Other which is inevitably engendered by the cognitive machinery that underpins the moral uprightness and pragmatic effectiveness inherent in the sense of responsibility to act. And as White understands the sense of responsibility to act and the sense of responsibility to otherness as mirroring two different ways of conceptualizing the

connection between human beings and language, he introduces a corresponding linguistic distinction. On the one hand, there is language that
functions among actors to "coordinate" those actions which fall under the
responsibility to act. On the other hand, language also can function to "dis-
close" the world, that is, to reveal the otherness and difference that is vic-
timized as it is created, ordered, and mastered by subjects obedient to the
prior sense of responsibility to act. "World-disclosing" language loosens
the hold of that sense of responsibility, as well as the hold of the "dominant
modes of identity and action coordination connected with it."

In line with the terms of Habermas's theory, White locates the sense of
responsibility to act and the understanding of language as a medium for
coordinating action as part of the "deep structure of modern Western styles
of thinking about ethics and politics." It is because Habermas takes this
ethical sense and its corresponding normative features of language as constituting an essential structural dimension of modern linguistic systems
that he can privilege the responsibility to act and its linguistic function. It
is ethical, in other words, to act *in the world.* And it is *responsible* to contribute to the reproduction of social life by mastering the learning processes
this entails. And this, in Habermas's view, is precisely where postmodernism fails. Attentive to the insights afforded by Habermas's argument,
White accordingly acknowledges that the difficulty with the world-
disclosing power of language is that it cannot be confirmed by a problem-
solving practice that contributes to societal reproduction. It does not function
responsibly in the world to promote action, including political action,
which can be justified by its moral and practical aims and achievements.

But although sympathetic, White is not allied uncritically with Habermas's position. On the contrary, he places equal emphasis on the importance of the sense of responsibility to otherness and the world-disclosing
function of language as contrasting concepts which "go beyond traditional
moral reasoning in ways that seem to involve deeply aesthetic qualities."
As White explains, postmodern theorists who endorse this orientation to
the world can object to Habermas's privileging of their modernist conceptual
counterparts as simply arbitrary ways to construct the world. The privileged status of these modernist ethical categories is a fiction, the rationale
for which has been concealed or forgotten. And it is this forgetting, White
points out, that has the "effect of denying the otherness that is spawned by
any human construct." Language, regardless of how it is construed, cannot

provide any ultimate support for one form of the reproduction of social life over any other. It is only the world-disclosing power of language that can illuminate the many ways in which the world is structured through language, how the contingent nature of social constructions have been forgotten, and by so doing loosen the grip of these structures on our thought and action so that we may become more sensitive to the otherness which they engender.

Whereas Habermas informs White's conceptualization of the sense of responsibility to act, it is Heidegger's thought that largely provides the philosophical arguments according to which White construes the sense of responsibility to otherness. Essentially, White draws heavily from Habermas and Heidegger to mount conceptual distinctions which enable him to force into confrontation modernist and postmodernist approaches to ethics and politics. As White contends,

> one can see that there is what looks like an irrevocable tension between the two orientations [represented by Heidegger and Habermas]. One can also understand why each orientation produces a specific recurrent critique of the other. The [sense of responsibility to otherness] is charged with an irresponsible, apolitical aestheticism, as it plays with the world-disclosing capacity of language and shows no theoretically informed way toward collective action; alternatively, it is charged with secretly desiring an aestheticized politics that exhibits a dangerous neglect of the distinction between, say, works of art and political action. . . . [In the other direction] political reflection pursued under the pull of a responsibility to act is charged with conceptual imperialism that is blind to its harmful practical consequences.[3]

While in the course of his argument White may at times appear to gravitate, to some small degree, toward the responsibility to act and the action-coordinating function of language, this is not because he sides with Habermas's position, but rather because his point of departure is his deeper interest in engaging certain traditional ethical-political questions. Overall, it is readily apparent that White wants to think about the implications of confronting both sides on equal terms and to avoid privileging one over and against the other. The entire thrust of his book is to preserve the tension between the responsibility to act and the responsibility to otherness, the action-coordinating and world-disclosing functions of language, and he does this precisely to demonstrate the consequences of allowing one position to be privileged unilaterally.

White's effort is all the more admirable for another reason. Heidegger's philosophy is not so textured that it in any way allows opposing views to be kept in the sort of proximity that can sustain the tension for which White aims. White is thus forced to work against the grain of Heidegger's arguments to keep them within the compass of the ethical-political questions to which he directs Heidegger to speak. White pursues this strategy by focusing, for the greatest part, on the explication of the concept of "finitude" found in Heidegger's later works. With this concept he forces Habermas and Heidegger into a discursive relation that poignantly clarifies how their positions are so inextricably bound together (without being reducible to one another), that we cannot take up the strengths and weaknesses of one without at the same time keeping those of the other in sight.

It is one of the boldest and most eloquent moments of White's argument when he declares that "within Habermas's framework we are creatures who seek to manipulate things in the world, to understand one another, and to get out from under domination, but *we are not creatures who die.*"[4] With this move White uncovers evidence of a gap in Habermas's framework that looms so large that it prevents him from being responsive to our need for making out our lives to be finite. Through its obsession with coordination, control, and mastery of that which lies actually or potentially within its ever encompassing eminent domain, modernity encourages us to forget that there are *limits* to our existence. But this is exactly what Habermas cannot acknowledge, for the responsibility to act, which he does privilege, and with which mastery is intimately associated, facilitates this forgetting, this "unlearning of our finitude." By relearning the finitude which modernity has compelled us to unlearn, we likewise unlearn the will to mastery. We posture ourselves in relation to a world that is then before and apart from—"other" than—the way it stands as an object to be mastered. As White argues, by again bearing witness to our own limits, to our own finitude, we would develop an attentive concern for the world's otherness, a responsiveness and responsibility to otherness which can take the form of resettling everyday life with a new mode of experience. Through recognition of our finitude we can come to face the world differently.

If the responsibility to otherness grows out of relearning our finitude, what makes this responsiveness to finitude possible? How do we bear witness to our own limits? How do we take up the posture toward otherness which allows the other to *be* in its difference? To take up this posture,

White explains, is to sense the fragility of the world, and such a sense of finitude, in Heidegger's view, is nurtured by the world-disclosing features of language, particularly by great poetry. In a creative move White piques our interest by suggesting that the linguistic qualities Heidegger celebrates may not be confined to poetry. Indeed, they may well extend to such works as Henry David Thoreau's *Walden,* which invokes the full range of moods associated with the sense and sensibility that allows us to be responsive and responsible to otherness. Coincidentally, White's intuitions will be confirmed by Jane Bennett's forthcoming contribution to **Modernity and Political Thought,** which reveals a spirit and sensitivity in Thoreau's work not unlike that which White discovers in Heidegger.

White's argument traces out the distance between the Heideggerian critique of the responsibility to act and those of other postmodern theorists. This is a distance that measures how successfully Heidegger's thought avoids the charge of aestheticism lodged against postmodern thinkers whose critiques occlude the possibility of conceptualizing a responsibility to otherness in ways which, in some sense, can be related to a consideration of other-oriented action in ethical-political terms. It is also a distance that shows the great extent to which postmodernism's genealogical and deconstructive strategies weaken the commitment to otherness and ethical-political reflections which would grow out of such a sustained commitment. Heidegger positions us to engage these commitments. By so doing he teaches us, in White's words, "how to situate ourselves in the *seam between* the aesthetic and the moral," even though Heidegger remains at some considerable distance from the ethical orientations entailed by the responsibility to act.[5] This seam is the thinking about otherness "into which flow both experiences with the world-disclosing or poetic dimension of language and the concern with finitude." It is a thinking which can thus take the form of resettling life with a new mode of experience. White's language expressing this achievement is itself beautifully world-disclosing when he affirms that Heidegger's commitment to finitude and otherness is "unequaled."

White's treatment of Heidegger offers a fascinating backdrop for *Edmund Burke: Modernity, Politics, and Aesthetics.* For White, Burke bears a striking resemblance to Heidegger. Virtually anticipating Heidegger's critique of the Enlightenment heritage, Burke sees what he refers to as the "modern system of morality and policy" as an *epochal* danger. Accordingly, Burke elaborates aesthetic categories which not only provide the terms with which he will reflect upon this entire problem but, most importantly, which appeal to modes of experience that might counter modernity's spirit of mastery. In this regard the similarity between the two thinkers is all the more remarkable. For Burke's conceptions of an "authentic sublime," referring to an experience that would revivify our sense of finitude and summarily deflate the modern urge to limitlessness, and of a perverted or "false sublime," which is identified with the urge to mastery and limitlessness, resonate deeply within Heidegger's work. And like Heidegger, Burke's hostility to modernity at times appears so pronounced that White can discover little in Burke that would enable us to think about how his appeals to alternative modes of experience might be related to the ethical concerns articulated by the responsibility to act.

Although the scholarly community often speaks of Burke as offering something like a "wisdom" about politics as opposed to a "theory," White prefers to argue for a reading of Burke's wisdom that revolves entirely around an ethics of the sublime conceived as a counterforce to modernity. This wisdom is not effortlessly drawn out of Burke. As White proves, one has to wrestle with it a bit to make it articulate. But White's labors have unearthed in Burke the sort of wisdom that loudly and startlingly echoes contemporary concerns. Edmund Burke thus perfectly complements the first four volumes of **Modernity and Political Thought.** For as do the contributions by William Connolly, Fred Dallmayr, Richard Flathman, and Michael Shapiro, Stephen White improves our understanding of what modernity is while also challenging us to speculate about what different cultural and political projects societies ought to pursue if the problems of modernity are to be overcome and its potential unlocked.

While there are many members of the Sage Publications editorial staff who have made **Modernity and Political Thought** possible, Carrie Mullen deserves special recognition for her hard work, creative attention to every stage of the production process, and, most importantly, for the professional support she has provided authors and editor alike. Her marks of excellence are imprinted on each volume.

—Morton Schoolman
State University of New York at Albany

Notes

1. Stephen K. White, *The Recent Work of Jürgen Habermas* (New York: Cambridge University Press, 1988).

2. Stephen K. White, *Political Theory and Postmodernism* (New York: Cambridge University Press, 1991).

3. Ibid, p. 28.

4. Ibid. p. 57 (my emphasis).

5. Ibid. p. 73 (my emphasis).

Acknowledgments

The research and writing of this book was generously supported by the National Endowment for the Humanities and the Center for Programs in the Humanities at Virginia Polytechnic Institute and State University. I am also grateful to Virginia Tech for a sabbatical year in 1990-1991, during which the project got under way.

Some of the ideas in the book were first sketched in "Burke on Politics, Aesthetics and the Dangers of Modernity," *Political Theory* 3 (August 1993). Versions of that paper were previously presented at the American Political Science Association meeting, August-September 1991, in Washington, D.C.; and at a meeting of the Conference for the Study of Political Thought, titled "After the Revolution: 1789-1848" at the University of Tulsa. Helpful criticism came from Alan Houston, Michael Mosher, and Tracy Strong. Thanks also are due to Timothy Luke, Donald Moon, and Morton Schoolman for reading the book manuscript as a whole. The last of these, in his role of series editor, deserves special gratitude for a lot of hard work and good judgment.

David Beagle in the Virginia Tech library was extremely helpful while I was doing the research. He is the model of what a librarian should be. The friendliness and superb skill of the secretaries in the Political Science

Department—Kim Hedge, Terry Kingrea, and Maxine Riley—made the preparation of the manuscript easier in countless ways. Finally, my family makes it all worthwhile: Pat, Lydia, and Cam. Besides being a wonderful partner, Pat helped as always with copyediting and French translations.

I also gratefully acknowledge permission from the publishers to cite passages from the following: *The Works of the Right Honorable Edmund Burke,* 12 vols. (Boston: Little, Brown, 1881); *The Writings and Speeches of Edmund Burke,* 5 vols. to date, edited by Paul Langford (Oxford: Clarendon Press, 1981-1991), by permission of Oxford University Press; and *The Correspondence of Edmund Burke,* 10 vols., edited by Thomas Copeland (Chicago: University of Chicago Press, 1958-1978).

1

Introduction

Edmund Burke is best known for his critique of the political rationalism and radicalism of the French Revolution, which he offered to the world in 1790, in *Reflections on the Revolution in France.*[1] For much of the twentieth century, the value of this critique has generally been found in the way it highlighted the dangers of revolutionary communism. According to Burke, such an ideology promises a better world, but ineluctably engenders regimes of violence and domination.

But the cold war is over. Communism in the now defunct Soviet Union and Eastern Europe has collapsed. It is no longer a threat, or at least not one of the same kind as before. Accordingly, Burke would seem to have lost his familiar role on our intellectual stage. If this is so, we have to begin rethinking Burke. Should we conclude that he can no longer really speak incisively to the issues that animate us at the close of the twentieth century? Should he be safely ensconced in the more exclusively historical wings of our stage?[2] Or can we discover ways in which he, like other major figures in the history of political thought, might still speak "directly" to us in some sense?

Some are quick to inform us that the latter strategy is easily open. Russell Kirk, for example, argues that Burke can help throw a much-

needed spotlight of interrogation on radical intellectuals within liberal democ-
racies. Such characters may live today in Manhattan instead of revolutionary Paris. But their aims remain the same: to corrode away all traditional
social restraints by the continued application of an acid of critical rationalism
that always extends the "empire of unnatural vices."[3] Although Kirk's suggestion may be warmly welcomed by some neoconservatives, it does not
do much justice to Burke. To pick only one "unnatural vice," during his
political career Burke went out of his way to plead for leniency in the
criminal punishment of homosexuals. Newspapers attacked him mercilessly
for this unpopular stand.[4] Clearly Burke is a more complicated figure than
Kirk would have us believe.

I. Burke's Multiple Languages

How one answers the question of what meaning—if any—Burke might
have for us today depends of course partially on what one thinks is at the
core of his political thinking. But this question is doubly difficult in Burke.
First, he wrote no major philosophical treatise, such as Locke's *Second
Treatise on Government* or Hobbes's *Leviathan*. Although his *Reflections
on the Revolution in France* is generally considered his most important
work, its having been composed as an extended letter makes it rather more
elusive and allusive than systematic and definitive. Burke was responding
in the *Reflections* to pressing, immediate circumstances. In fact, almost all
of his writings have this characteristic, which is hardly surprising given
the fact that he was an active politician for the better part of his adult life.

A second difficulty in interpreting Burke is that his arguments are often
couched in more than one idiom or "language game," with no clear priority
granted to any. For example, near the end of his political life Burke wrote
a short essay entitled "Thoughts and Details on Scarcity," in which he
argued that political interference with markets should not be attempted.[5]
The year 1795 was one of substantial hardship for the agricultural poor in
England, and various possible remedies were being discussed. In some
locales a policy of supplementing low wages out of public coffers had been
established. In this essay, there is no ambivalence whatsoever as to *where*
Burke stands on the merits of such a policy; however, when one tries to

decide exactly *why* he adopted his stance, things are not so easy. Burke speaks within several language games, each of which on its own might have been adequate to justify his position. To a point, he argues like his friend Adam Smith that one should not interfere with the "invisible hand" operating in free markets; to do so ultimately will interfere with growing material prosperity. But he also asserts that this hand is controlled by a greater one, that of God; in effect, the laws of supply and demand are divinely ordained. As he argues, "the laws of commerce . . . are the laws of Nature, and consequently the laws of God."[6] The language of natural law in Burke is related not just to the language of economics, but also to that of the "Great Chain of Being," according to which all creation is linked through relationships of superior and subordinate. The activity of agriculture is part of "a natural and just order: the beast is as an informing principle to the plough and cart; the laborer is as reason to the beast; and the farmer is as a thinking and presiding principle to the laborer." Any attempt "to break this chain of subordination" is "absurd."[7]

At this point, one might think that the argument is already pretty overdetermined. Burke, however, brings another language to bear, that of tradition. He contends that the taxes that support supplemental wages constitute an "arbitrary" seizure of property, thus infringing on the traditions of English common law.[8]

But even this is not enough. Burke's trump language here, as in so much of his later writings, is a language of fear—fear of revolutionary violence. One means of combating the high price of foodstuffs was through the construction of public granaries. The idea was that these might help prevent the upward manipulation of grain prices. For Burke, however, they would merely become sites of "popular frenzy" aimed at a government that would never be able to keep prices low enough to satisfy the poor.[9] Such had been the experience of France. Burke no doubt knew this, as did the prime minister, the younger William Pitt, to whom Burke sent his essay. Such granaries would become English seedbeds of Jacobin violence and anarchy. For a government that had seen the king's carriage stoned by an angry crowd on the way back from the opening of Parliament only a month before, Burke's specter was hardly a remote threat.

How does an interpreter of Burke decide which language is primary? Is it the language of tradition and prescription? of classical natural law (in Aquinas's sense)? of classical political economy? or of revolutionary fear?

These struggles have been the traditional bread and butter of Burke scholars. Of course, to speak of a language of fear as a distinct phenomenon in Burke's texts is perhaps not really legitimate. A language of fear is effective in politics only if it is connected with a more articulated language, such as one of the others just mentioned. The question then becomes: Were Burke's "horrible pictures" (as Tom Paine called them) intended primarily to evoke fear that traditions were crumbling, that the natural order was threatened, or, as C. B. Macpherson has argued, that the conditions for "capitalist accumulation" were being disturbed?[10] Actually, Burke probably thought all of these things were in danger of occurring. However, one must nevertheless ask which of these more articulated languages best accounts for the depth and intensity of Burke's fear of what the French Revolution represented. For example, concerns over the conditions of capitalist accumulation or inflated currency hardly seem adequate to account for the following sentiments, expressed by a gravely ill Burke a few months before he died. He confides in a letter to a friend that the French Revolution "is a subject, which I cannot contemplate, even, at the moment of my probable departure, without a deeper interest than I ought perhaps to take in any human affairs."[11]

This existential depth of concern on Burke's part is one thing that makes the natural law approach to his work perennially attractive. It tells us, in short, that Burke's fear was so deep because he saw the God-ordained, moral structure of the world itself threatened with destruction. And yet, if one decides to give priority to the language of classical natural law, one has to be puzzled by the fact that as numerous commentators have noted, Burke's talk about that law tends to have a fairly rhetorical and platitudinous quality to it.[12] It is difficult not to feel that the real force of the analysis in Burke's texts is being carried by other languages.

One recently suggested way of resolving the question of multiple languages in Burke is to recast him as primarily a rhetorician.[13] This Burke is interested only in the practical shaping of political opinion into whatever form he finds that circumstances demand. From such a rhetorical perspective, one can easily understand why "Burke was never content to deploy one argument where he could use two or three."[14] Philosophical consistency always took a back seat to political effect.

Although there is much insight to be gained from emphasizing the rhetorical side of Burke, it nevertheless tends to blend out too radically certain features of his work. This is especially true in regard to his confrontation with modernity, or better, *political* modernity, by which I mean his perception that he was witnessing a systematic explosion of willfulness in politics that had a world historical significance. One loses too much of a sense of the intensity of Burke's struggle against this phenomenon when one reduces it merely to one of many political subjects upon which he exercised his considerable rhetorical skills.

What I want to suggest in this book is that this issue is best brought to life if we attend to a language in Burke that I have not so far mentioned. An understanding of Burke's use of this language will enable one to account for the depth of his fear, to see how his analysis of political modernity as a whole takes shape, and finally to consider to what degree there is any abiding wisdom in this analysis. The language I am referring to is an aesthetic one of the sublime and beautiful, and of the human affections or sentiments associated with them. Its basic grammar is set out in *A Philosophical Inquiry Into the Origins of our Ideas of the Sublime and Beautiful,* written in 1757, before Burke's political career began.[15]

It may initially seem surprising that I would relate an aesthetic language to Burke's deepest fears about the structure of the world. But one must remember that today we are used to thinking of aesthetics as a far more narrow and distinct area of inquiry than it was in Burke's time. In fact, the term "aesthetics" did not appear in English until about 1800.[16] The aesthetic, or better, aesthetic-affective, dimension was always for Burke closely intertwined with the character of the natural, divinely ordained structure of the world. Moreover, whereas his thinking about the latter was basically unoriginal, his reflections on the former are quite original and help to shape many of his most distinctive political insights.

I will not be trying to claim that an aesthetic-affective language is *the* key language that unlocks the true meaning of Burke. However, I do think we fail to understand fully how he construed political modernity and its dangers unless we attend more carefully to this language. This issue returns us directly to the question of Burke's contemporary meaning. Even if his attack on the emergence of democratic politics in the eighteenth century contains much that is patently unappealing today, we may yet find that as we try to assess the ambiguous legacy of modernity, Burke's peculiar interrelating of aesthetics and politics is eminently worth our serious attention. Stated most generally, what I am referring to here is the way in which Burke shares with many contemporary thinkers a deeply hostile attitude toward the figure of the self-determining, rational subject who conceives of himself as the master of all he surveys. In both cases there is an attempt to illuminate the perils facing this modern master who envisions his background and foreground as merely temporary limits to his willful designs. By "background" and "foreground" I mean those things that constitute, as it were, the "others" of the self-determining, rational individual: the affective, the bodily, the intersubjective, the traditional.

When Burke considered these contextual bounds of individual mastery, he did so in a fashion that kept aesthetic reflections intimately entangled with moral-political concerns. For Burke, to speak of what we think of as the distinct sphere of aesthetics was also necessarily to speak of power, gender, moral sentiment, tradition, and social hierarchy. This connection is crucial for present concerns. It should be noted, moreover, that it is just such entwinement that was rejected—authoritatively for modern philosophy—by Kant. Although Kant was impressed by Burke's analysis of the sublime, he modified his own account in such a way that it fit easily into his overall separation of the spheres of the cognitive, the moral, and the aesthetic. But perhaps Burke was on to something. Many contemporary critics are certainly skeptical of Kant's policy of radical divorce. The current vogue for reexamining that philosopher's aesthetics (in his *Critique of Judgment*) for hints toward new ways of conceptualizing ethics might also lend some collateral legitimacy to reexamining the comparable insights of Burke.

Given these considerations, I will suggest that Burke's notion of the sublime should not be considered, as it usually is, simply as a stepping-stone toward Kant; on the contrary, it may be a better notion, at least in its relation to moral-political reflection. Kant's sublime ultimately reduces to an affective experience, the main value of which lies in getting us to marvel at how elevated the human moral will is above the world of social and natural phenomena.[17] It thus puts primary emphasis on our participation in the infinite, in the noumenal world. In conceiving of the sublime in this way, Kant unwittingly involves himself in a "humanizing" of the sublime, something that Burke finds to be at the heart of what disturbs him about the mix of will and politics in modernity.

One of the distinct dangers courted in any attempt to unearth some wisdom in Burke's aesthetics is that of becoming entangled with the oppressive account of gender he endorses throughout his writings. In the *Inquiry,* Burke sketched an affinity between, on the one hand, the sublime and beautiful, and on the other hand, male and female, public and private. He modified this bipolar perspective somewhat in later years, but it always retained enough force to keep him adamantly opposed to a change in women's roles. He was first called to task by Mary Wollstonecraft in 1790 for this use of aesthetic categories to help reify traditional views of women.[18] Such critique has never ceased, and for patently good reasons. But perhaps one can sufficiently qualify an affirmation of Burke's notion of the sublime such that it no longer plays this gendered role. That at least is my hope.[19]

As I said earlier, any interpretation of Burke must begin with particular attention to the circumstances in which he lived and wrote. Thus, in what remains of this chapter, I will sketch an outline of his life. This will form the basis for the more specific insights I develop in the following chapters.

II. Biographical Sketch

Burke was born in 1729 in Dublin. At this time in Ireland, Catholics faced a forbidding array of restrictions on such things as property ownership, access to professions, and political participation. Burke's father was a moderately successful attorney who apparently had converted to Protestantism only a few years before Edmund was born. The conversion was likely a matter of expedience, and the Protestant authorities looked upon such people with a good deal of suspicion. Edmund's mother remained a Catholic throughout her life. The young boy's sense of the oppressive conditions in his country was likely intensified in his primary school years, because he was sent during that time to his mother's relatives in a strongly Catholic area outside of Dublin.[20] At the age of 12, he was transferred to a Quaker school at Ballitore in Queen's County. There he was given a thorough grounding in the classics and prepared for university education. Although it is of course difficult to speculate about such things, it seems likely that this phase of his education induced Burke to reflect upon oppression in a broader cultural and historical context and to consider religious intolerance of any sort to be reprehensible.

Burke always gave the impression of being an ambitious and talented individual, and at Trinity College in Dublin he immersed himself in academic and cultural life. While still an undergraduate in 1748, he launched a journal called the *The Reformer,* in which he held forth on a variety of social, political, and aesthetic topics. The strong relationship Burke saw between aesthetics and moral-political ideas was already apparent here. One of the main aims of the *The Reformer,* he announced in its first issue, was to reform public sentiments and morality by means of criticism of theatrical performances in Dublin. In other issues, he took on questions of political life more directly. One notable essay strongly censured the upper classes for their laziness, lack of public-spiritedness, and failure to show pity for the poor. His suggested remedy was for landowners to become more active and efficient managers, as a result of which both they and their laborers would become materially better off. Reform and improvement would come within the existing order by each person better fulfilling the duties proper to his or her place in the great chain of existence.[21]

This desire for improvement counterbalanced by a concern to contain it within an existing order is one manifestation of perhaps the most resilient tension in Burke's mind. He always sought to give encouragement to talents and ambition (his own included), but he also desired somehow to keep them within limits. The problem of chastening human willfulness was not something Burke discovered only when he confronted revolutionary zeal later in life. "Humility," he asserted during his stay at Trinity, is "the greatest of Christian virtues." A few years later, he added: "Whatever tends to humble us, tends to make us wiser."[22]

After college, in 1750, Burke traveled to London to study law. He never was entirely comfortable with this career path, but his father was set on it. He dutifully pursued his studies for a while, but gave them up eventually. During this time, he met another law student, William Burke (no relation), who was to remain an intimate friend throughout his life. The two often traveled about the countryside in bohemian style, apparently seeking to put as much physical and mental space between themselves and the law as possible. Burke's state of mind at this time is nicely expressed in one of his notebooks. It contains an entry that begins with legal notes and ends with drafts of poetry.[23] These two sides of Burke finally found ample synthetic expression in his later career as a parliamentary orator. Perhaps no one in the English language has ever matched his output of speeches and writings when it comes to combining a careful attention to complex issues and voluminous factual material, on the one hand, with such a density of vivid imagery, on the other.

There is a dearth of information on Burke during the early 1750s. He appears to have suffered some sort of mental breakdown, from which he was nursed back to health in the home of a physician named Christopher Nugent. He married Nugent's daughter Jane in 1757. During the later part of the decade he also was rapidly developing his literary skills. His first emergence into the public eye came in 1756, with his publication of *A Vindication of Natural Society*.[24] It was a satire on the then-popular writings of Lord Bolingbroke. Burke's intention was to demonstrate the ridiculousness of thinking that social and political life could be understood and justified purely by the light of our reason. Burke's real fame, however, began with the appearance, a year later, of *A Philosophical Inquiry Into the Origins of Our Ideas of the Sublime and the Beautiful*. This has been called the "most influential" discussion of the sublime in English in the eighteenth century.[25] One indication of this is that over thirty years later, when Burke wrote the *Reflections,* his critics were quick to draw connections between that work and the *Inquiry*. Mary Wollstonecraft, for example, berated Burke for his treatment of women in both places.[26] Another sort of negative sentiment was expressed in a pamphlet felicitously entitled, "The Wonderful Flights of Edmund the Rhapsodist into the Sublime and Beautiful regions of Fancy, Fiction, Extravagance, and Absurdity, exposed and laughed at."[27]

Burke's literary fame was such that in 1764 he was included among the founding members of perhaps the most famous literary club in eighteenth-century England. Its small circle included Samuel Johnson, Sir Joshua Reynolds, Oliver Goldsmith, and the actor and impresario David Garrick. Others, such as Adam Smith, joined in later years. "The Club," as it was called, met weekly (later monthly) for dinner and conversation. By agreement the topics for discussion were literary, not political. Sir Joshua Reynolds became Burke's closest friend (apart from William Burke). The eminent painter's high opinion of his friend's knowledge of aesthetics is reflected in his turning to Burke for critical comment on the rough drafts of the famous discourses on art that Reynolds delivered to the Royal Academy of Art in the late 1760s.[28]

Burke's accomplishments in satire and aesthetics should not lead one to think that his early interests were narrowly literary. During this same period, there is some evidence that he was earning money as a pamphlet and speech writer for different political figures.[29] Moreover, in 1758, he undertook the editorship of the newly established *Annual Register*. This review, for which Burke did almost all of the writing for the first few years, covered not only current developments in literature, drama, and art, but also political events and philosophy.[30] Here he reviewed the work of contemporary thinkers such as Rousseau and Adam Smith. Simultaneously Burke embarked on a full-scale history of England. Although he abandoned the project pretty quickly, he nevertheless completed a manuscript of some 300 pages.[31] His knowledge of history and politics is further evidenced by his deep involvement with William Burke's *An Account of the European Settlements in America*. Although Edmund Burke probably did not write the entire book, as some have argued, he did apparently do a substantial amount of the writing and editing.[32]

In sum, by 1765, when Burke embarked on his parliamentary career at the age of 36, he was already a man of remarkably broad intellect. One commentator has gone so far as to call him "one of the best informed men in England."[33] It is important to emphasize this in the present context because political theorists have traditionally downplayed Burke's early work, especially the *Inquiry*. Burke's own later biting remarks about the uselessness, and even dangerousness, of "metaphysical" speculation and professorial approaches to the world of politics would seem to lend some credence to this custom of interpretation, because the *Inquiry* certainly has the air of a scholarly treatise about it. I want to suggest, however, that Burke's aesthetic ideas were not juvenilia, later set aside or at best drawn upon for rhetorical purposes in his mature writings. It is true that Burke seems to have worked on some of the basic ideas of the *Inquiry* as early as his undergraduate years. However, those ideas were only brought to fruition and tested in public discussion in the late 1750s and early 1760s, a time during which Burke was developing an extraordinary range of intellectual competence. The basic fabric of his mind was woven during this period, and an essential part of its design was aesthetic. In saying this, I am not asserting that all of Burke's later ideas are already present. Rather, only that his aesthetic ideas are at this point interwoven with his broader reflections on the social and political world, and that this remains the case to the end of his life. Of course, the proof of the last part of this claim can only be demonstrated by actually interpreting the later texts, as I will do. The main thing at this point is simply to see that the traditional strategy of largely setting aside Burke's youthful and "apolitical" work is highly problematic.

In 1759, Burke began a sustained relationship as personal secretary with William Hamilton, a young member of Parliament. In 1761, Hamilton was named chief secretary to the Lord Lieutenant of Ireland, Lord Halifax. The Lord Lieutenant was the chief agent of the English government in Ireland. Burke was now deeply immersed in political life, and his initial intention of preserving substantial time for his literary activities became increasingly difficult to sustain. This tension led finally to a break between employer and employee. Within a short time, however, Burke's name was put forward as a possible private secretary to the Marquess of Rockingham. This immensely wealthy Whig leader had been named by the king to head a new administration in 1765. Burke was given the secretarial position, and shortly thereafter one of Rockingham's well-heeled supporters arranged for Burke to be elected a member of Parliament from a seat he controlled. Thus began a remarkable political career that was to last the better part of three decades. And from this point on as well, the "literary" Burke recedes into private life. By this I do not mean that his later writings do not have literary qualities; in fact, just the opposite is the case. His rhetorical flair and his facility with classical allusions are well known. What I mean is that Burke's public political reflections do not in any explicit, systematic way incorporate his aesthetic language. Burke was now a public figure and his writings were aimed primarily at persuading politically influential people. Arguments couched in aesthetic language were hardly likely to sit well with this audience.

But this shift should not be taken as evidence of a rejection of any real intellectual substance. Rather it seems far more plausible to see it as an eminently prudent step to take for an outsider who had just been catapulted into the higher circles of political life. Here one must always remember how persistently the seam between inside and outside was a source of pain for Burke. Critics denigrated him as an Irish adventurer and a man of no independent property; they also hinted that he was a secret agent of the Jesuits. An additional charge that was directed at him early on helps to give one some sense as to why he would not wish to appear too literary to the political leaders around him. One of the nobility wrote to the former prime minister, Lord Grenville, that Burke had a disturbing degree of influence on Rockingham. He went on to describe the newcomer as "descended from a garret . . . a metaphysician, a man of great learning and imagination." Although "a garret is a very proper situation for those who mean to read the stars," it is hardly an appropriate one for those who must conduct the practical affairs of nations.[34] No doubt Burke was aware of such criticism. It is thus hardly surprising that he should choose to give no additional ammunition on this score to his enemies.[35]

This shift to a less explicitly literary posture was probably not felt by Burke as any real psychological burden. The renown that came with prominence in Parliament was no doubt a source of immense pleasure to him. And after all, he still had private access to a more lively cultural milieu through his circle of friends in The Club. In addition, as his fame grew, he was always a welcome guest at the literary gatherings of some of London's most eminent "bluestocking" hostesses, such as Mrs. Montagu and Mrs. Vesey.[36] In short, my highlighting of the shift in Burke's life at this point is not intended to suggest that he had to repress anything; rather it is intended only to help explain why he quite reasonably kept his aesthetic reflections off the publicly printed page.

Rockingham's ministry fell less than a year after it had come to power. He did not return to lead an administration for almost two decades. But it was in this interim that Burke rose to prominence as a clever political adviser and one of the top orators in Parliament. During this period, Rockingham played the role of Whig opposition leader, and Burke did everything he could to help provide this opposition with a coherent set of principles. He was especially concerned to call attention to what he felt was a dangerous increase in the influence of the Crown in politics, a tendency considered threatening to the distribution of constitutional power between the Commons, Lords, and king that had been accepted after the Glorious Revolution in 1688.

Already in 1768, Burke felt confident enough about his prospects to purchase a small country estate at Beaconsfield. The dream of becoming an independent man of property and a successful manager of an estate remained, however, always out of reach. His purchase saddled him with debts from which he never recovered and about which he was often acutely embarrassed.

Burke's star continued to rise, and in 1774, he entered and won a contested parliamentary race for a seat from the important commercial city of Bristol. The struggle with the American colonies was increasingly pushing to the fore at this point. Burke and the opposition continually hammered away at what they found to be the ineptitude and heavy-handedness of the administration of Lord North in its negotiations with the colonists. The American Revolution, he felt, was eminently avoidable. And when it came, he thought of it not as the dawning of an *age* of revolution, but rather simply as a major policy failure for the British Empire.

As the war dragged on and Great Britain's likelihood of losing became increasingly apparent, the Whig opposition felt that sooner or later they would return to power. And in 1782, Rockingham and his allies did just that. Burke was at the height of his career and was responsible for drafting and passing a major piece of reform legislation designed to economize on administration and curtail the power of the Crown. The personal and party success that seemed to be the just deserts of so many years of hard work in opposition evaporated very quickly, however, with the death of Rockingham after only a few months in office. Burke was now left without his patron. In addition, his financial affairs had just taken a turn for the worse.

The dimming of Burke's hopes for himself and his party probably hastened a subtle shift that had recently appeared in his political reflections. During the 1760s and 1770s, he had held fast to the belief that if men of principle and sound policy could only get hold of the reins of government, then any serious problems would be alleviated. In 1780, Burke began to think differently about some of the events he was witnessing. He started to see them not as occasional but *epochal,* in the sense that he felt it likely they would become more frequent and gather momentum. In short, Burke was beginning to see political modernity as an imposing force. He would spend the remainder of his life trying to fathom it and perceive ways in which it could be combated, at least in its worst excesses.

In the early part of 1780, proposals for the reform of Parliament were being put forward. Some were for more frequent elections, others were for an extension of the franchise. At first, Burke showed no particular enthusiasm for such proposals and the popular agitation associated with them; but he also did not express adamant hostility. In general, he preferred specific remedies for specific complaints. As he so often said, prudence and

attention to "circumstances" were paramount. But he indicated nevertheless that larger, constitutional changes might be made if plenty of time
were allowed for debate, and if it became clear that "a decided majority of
the people wanted" them.[37]

Burke's skepticism toward popular will in politics soon ripened into a
hostility that was to become a source of both deep insight as well as extraordinary blindness in his later writings. One well-known event hasten-
ing Burke's change of attitude was the loss of his seat at Bristol near the
end of 1780. He had clashed with the electorate over the question of whether
a representative should follow the explicit directions of his constituents or
exercise his judgment more independently.[38] Burke took the latter position. What is of some importance in the present context is the fact that he
and his friends blamed the loss of his seat on the bad judgment and willfulness of the "lower" or common people who supported his opponents.[39]

This event, however, was probably not the crucial one in Burke's change
of mind. That role was more likely played by the Gordon Riots in June
1780. Anyone who encounters Burke's writings on the French Revolution
is struck by the way he associates any popular agitation in the streets with
images of humanity gone mad. The depth and thoroughness of this association are rooted in these earlier disturbances that Burke experienced first
hand. The Gordon Riots lasted for a week. Numerous people were killed
and the destruction of property was staggering. Some sense of the magnitude of the riots can be gained by a comparison with revolutionary Paris.
It has been estimated that the property damage in London during this one
week was ten times that in Paris during the course of the whole revolution.[40] Burke's own home was attacked and he was forced to wield a sword
in self-defense.[41]

The riots were not the work of supporters of parliamentary reform. Rather
they had a distinctly reactionary tone. Parliament had recently taken modest steps toward greater toleration of Catholics in England. It was this direction of public policy that Lord Gordon and his supporters were attacking.
And Burke, always suspected in the popular press of being a secret "Pop-
ish" agent, was a prominent target of the speeches that incited the crowd.[42]

Thus, the riots were clearly more backward than forward looking. This,
of course, makes it somewhat strange that Burke would allow the riots to
become so inextricably linked in his mind with the emergence of a new
political epoch. In speaking of reform proposals only a month before the

riots, Burke soberly warned of the unintended consequences of large-scale political change. One of these was the likelihood of inflaming a "violent and furious popular spirit."[43] Perhaps Burke simply saw the Gordon Riots as evidence that such a spirit could quickly infect others who had no connection with the reform proposals. There is also the fact that Burke, at this time, probably saw both sorts of upheavals as linked because of their likelihood of undermining the independence of Parliament, thus aiding the expansion of the Crown's influence.[44]

Although the precise reason that Burke connected the riots of 1780 with the drive for political reform may not be clear, the fact that he did cannot be denied. Over a decade later, in surveying the effects of the French Revolution and what he felt to be the rapidly growing danger of English Jacobinism, Burke stated unequivocally that their roots lay in the "spirit" of the Gordon Riots.[45] The spirit is that of what I am calling *political modernity.* My use of this term is not as anachronistic as it might seem. Although Burke never used this precise term, it would not have puzzled him. In the same work of 1793 in which he identified this spirit's origins, he also referred to its full embodiment in France as "the modern system of morality and policy."[46]

My contention is that already in the early 1780s, Burke had begun to sense that a distinctive creature was afoot on the historical stage, and that it presented traditional political life with a clear and present danger. (I will flesh this interpretation out in Chapter 3.) Burke even went so far as to suggest in his "Fourth Letter on a Regicide Peace" (1795), that it was not the French Revolution that initially caused rebellious dissatisfaction in England; on the contrary, it was rather the "speculative faction" in England in the early 1780s that give birth to the disease that came to plague France![47] It was in his own country that he first sensed clearly the potential explosiveness of an unbound popular will, animated by philosophical speculation and turned upon an existing constitutional order. Referring to the "wild and savage insurrection" that "prowled our streets in the name of Reform" in the early 1780s, Burke suggests that if such reforms had been enacted at that time, then "not France, but England, would have had the honor of leading up the death-dance of democratic revolution."[48]

Rockingham's death in July 1782 was an immense blow to Burke. The Whig party also was thrown into a long period of decline. Within a year, the king threw his support for prime minister to one of Burke's adamant

opponents, the younger William Pitt. Moreover, the Whigs lost badly in
the elections of 1784, a result Burke attributed to a "felonious act" of the
people.[49] As Burke's political dreams evaporated, his family finances went
from bad to worse. In sum, the better part of the decade was "an endless
series of embarrassments" for him.[50] The famed orator even found himself
heckled and his speeches laughed at by many of the younger members of
Parliament.

It is during this period of decline that Burke's interest in British rule in
India turned into what can only be called an obsession. Burke's outrage at
the corrupt and oppressive rule of the East India Company, then directed
by Governor General Warren Hastings, grew steadily during the 1780s.
Many in Parliament agreed that the company's behavior had to be reformed,
but no others worked as hard to inform themselves fully on Indian affairs
or pressed as persistently for the impeachment of Hastings as Burke. Impeachment was voted by the House of Commons in 1787, and the trial
before the Lords began the following year. Burke delivered the opening
speech and presented many of the charges in this trial that dragged on until
Hastings's final acquittal in 1795.

Burke's obsession with bringing the "captain general in iniquity" to justice can only partially be explained by Hastings's actual wrongdoing.[51] It
seems likely that Burke saw the impeachment as his last chance to make a
permanent mark on British politics, a mark he might now make in his own
right, without a patron. But as the proceedings developed, Burke came to
realize that the Lords would not vote for conviction. It could not be shown
that Hastings had violated any English law, and preliminary procedural
rulings made it clear that the Lords were unlikely to accept the argument
that Hastings had violated natural law, as Burke and his fellow managers
tried to show. A great empire could not be administered effectively when
such a diffuse, but potentially exacting, standard could suddenly be brought
to bear.

Even if much of Burke's excessive zeal can be explained by his desire
to secure a personal place in British history, it nevertheless remains true
that he also saw British rule in India as succumbing to what he was coming
to understand as a further dimension of the threat of political modernity.
Thus, the stakes in the Indian question were ultimately no different from
those raised by the French Revolution. Burke often referred to "Indianism
and Jacobinism" as "the two great Evils of our time."[52] By "Indianism,"

Burke meant to some degree merely a virulent strain of tyranny; at times he compared the oppressiveness of the East India Company with that of the Protestant Ascendancy in Ireland.[53] But he also meant more, for in the figures of Hastings and his lieutenants Burke saw a phenomenon of human willfulness that was not adequately comprehended by the traditional categories of tyranny or despotism.

If in the early 1780s, it was the face of the tumultuous people that most worried Burke, it was now the face of the new "entrepreneurs" of modernity that drew his attention. Some commentators have seen Burke's whole life as an embodiment of the strains generated in the eighteenth century between the demands of the rising class of bourgeois men of talents and the restraints of a traditional, aristocratic order.[54] I think what ended up fascinating Burke about India was that it represented a kind of controlled, sociomoral experiment with men of talent. The experiment raised the question: What is likely to happen when individuals of talent but no property are given political power without any effective controls by the church or the established elite in Parliament? The results of the experiment were not encouraging. Such men exhibited an overwhelming ambitiousness and rapaciousness that made life in various areas of India extremely oppressive. Burke elaborated upon their misdeeds in great detail in the articles of impeachment. Hastings, then, became in Burke's mind a modern archetype; in effect, the unscrupulous land "developer." This character, however, only comes to play his full role when he joins forces with the metaphysical, "political architect."[55] It was this dangerous alliance that Burke was soon to see taking shape in the French Revolution.

When revolutionary events began in 1789, Burke was at first watchful and cautious in his assessment. But within a few months, he began to have grave doubts. A young French supporter of the revolution wrote to the aging English politician at this time in the hope that the latter would endorse the new political course. But Burke's doubts only deepened as he began his reply. This letter expanded rapidly and finally emerged in November 1790 as *Reflections on the Revolution in France.*

The vehemence of Burke's attack stunned many of his acquaintances, even those who shared doubts about the revolution. For sympathizers, Burke became a hated figure. A torrent of pamphlets were written to refute his claims. Burke never wavered for a minute in his stance. His intransigence soon began to make life within the Whig party increasingly difficult. One of the party's ascending stars at the time was Charles William Fox. His faction of the party was distinctly favorable to the ideas of the revolution. Within a year Burke broke publicly with Fox and soon after published his "Appeal From the New to the Old Whigs," in which he excoriated his opponent's supporters for breaking with the traditions of the party.[56]

Increasingly isolated politically, Burke and his son Richard kept up active contacts with the French emigré community throughout Europe, hoping in some way to help promote a counterrevolution. With the declaration of war by France on England, the guillotining of the French king, and the beginning of the Terror in 1793, Burke had reason to think that perhaps his countrymen would finally recognize the magnitude of the danger. Although there was certainly a shift in public opinion, Burke never felt it to be adequate. In his last years, he incessantly complained that the war was not being prosecuted vigorously enough, and the government was not unequivocally committed to the ultimate goal of extirpating Jacobinism from the face of the earth. And when the government extended peace feelers in 1795, Burke, now retired from Parliament, fired off his "Letters on a Regicide Peace."[57] No peace, short of one following total victory, would satisfy him.

Although Burke wrote and advised political leaders about various matters during the 1790s, he approached all issues in the same way. As he wrote in a letter in 1795: "My whole politics, at present, center in one point; and to this the merit or demerit of every measure . . . is referable: that is, what will most promote or depress the cause of Jacobinism?"[58]

In the months leading up to his death in July 1797, Burke saw no reason for anything but pessimism about the likelihood of defeating the revolutionary danger. The Jacobins, he worried, would pursue him even after death. As a final act of defiance, Burke arranged to have his body placed some distance from the grave marker. His pursuers would be allowed no opportunity to desecrate his remains.

Having sketched a broad picture of Burke's career and central concerns, I turn now to the question of the nature of his aesthetic language and how its conceptual resources led him to see political modernity as such a threatening phenomenon. In the next chapter, I consider the origins of Burke's aesthetics in his early work. Chapter 3 then shows how these early views helped structure his understanding of the political world after he entered Parliament. This political experience, however, also had a reciprocal effect on his aesthetic ideas during the 1760s, an effect which continued into the

1780s. A careful consideration of this mutual interplay of aesthetic and political reflections over many years is crucial for an adequate comprehension of the danger Burke found in the French Revolution. In Chapter 4, I take up this most famous of Burke's confrontations with political events and show how he came to understand that modern revolutionary consciousness is at least partially constituted by a sensibility for a "false sublime." In the concluding chapter, I ask whether this aesthetic dimension of Burke's critique of political modernity retains any resonance for us today.

Notes

References to Burke's work will be cited as follows: The standard U.S. edition of his writings is *The Works of The Right Honorable Edmund Burke,* 12 vols. (Boston: Little, Brown, 1881); cited as *Works.* This and other old editions are being replaced by *The Writings and Speeches of Edmund Burke* (Oxford, U.K.: Clarendon Press), of which five volumes have appeared; cited as *WS.* Burke's correspondence is contained in *The Correspondence of Edmund Burke,* 10 vols. (Chicago: University of Chicago Press, 1958-1978); cited as *Corr.*

1. *WS,* VIII, pp. 53-293.

2. See, for example, C. B. Macpherson, *Burke* (New York: Hill & Wang, 1980), Chap. 6.

3. Russell Kirk, "Foreword" in *Edmund Burke: Appraisals and Applications,* ed. Daniel E. Ritchie (New Brunswick, NJ: Transaction, 1990), p. xi.

4. On the issue of homosexuality, see Isaac Kramnick, *The Rage of Edmund Burke: Portrait of an Ambivalent Conservative* (New York: Basic Books), 1977, pp. 83-87.

5. "Thoughts and Details on Scarcity," *Works,* V, pp. 134-69.

6. Ibid., p. 157.

7. Ibid., p. 140.

8. Ibid., p. 137.

9. Ibid., p. 153.

10. Macpherson, *Burke,* p. 61.

11. *Corr.,* IX, p. 268.

12. Frank O'Gorman, *Edmund Burke: His Political Philosophy* (Bloomington: Indiana University Press, 1973), pp. 98, 104-5.

13. See F. P. Lock, *Burke's Reflections on the Revolution in France* (London: George Allen & Unwin, 1985), pp. 97-98, Chap. 3; and Ian Hampsher-Monk, "Rhetoric and Opinion in the Politics of Edmund Burke," *History of Political Thought* 9, 3 (Winter 1988): 455-84.

14. Lock, *Burke's Reflections,* p. 97.

15. *Works,* I, pp. 66-262.

16. The term "aesthetic" was first used in German by Alexander Baumgarten in the 1750s.

17. Immanuel Kant, *Critique of Judgment,* trans. with introduction by Werner S. Pluhar (Indianapolis, IN: Hackett, 1987), pp. 97-140. Cf. Stephen White, *Political Theory and Postmodernism* (Cambridge: Cambridge University Press, 1991), pp. 85-88, 89.

18. Mary Wollstonecraft, *A Vindication of the Rights of Men* (Delmar, NY: Scholar's Facsimiles and Reprints, 1975).

19. My approach has been criticized by Linda M.G. Zerrilli, "No Thrust, No Swell, No Subject? A Critical Response to Stephen K. White," *Political Theory* 22 (May 1994). See also my reply, "Desperately Seeking Marie?" in the same issue.

20. On the importance of Burke's Catholic upbringing, see Conor Cruise O'Brien, *The Great Melody: A Thematic Biography of Edmund Burke* (Chicago: University of Chicago Press, 1992), pp. 3-31.

21. Issues of *The Reformer* are reprinted in Arthur P. I. Samuels, *The Early Life, Correspondence and Writings of the Rt. Honorable Edmund Burke* (Cambridge: Cambridge University Press, 1923), pp. 316-17.

22. The first remark is quoted in Stanley Ayling, *Edmund Burke: His Life and Opinions* (New York: St. Martin's, 1988), p. 5; the second remark appears in *A Notebook of Edmund Burke,* ed. H.V.F. Somerset (Cambridge: Cambridge University Press, 1957), p. 85.

23. *Corr.,* I, note 2, p. 105.

24. "A Vindication of Natural Society," *Works,* I, pp. 1-66.

25. Samuel Monk, *The Sublime: A Study of Critical Theories in XVIII-Century England,* 2nd ed. (Ann Arbor: University of Michigan Press, 1950), p. xi.

26. *A Vindication of the Rights of Man* (Gainesville: University of Florida Press, 1960).

27. Cited in "Editor's Introduction" in Edmund Burke, *A Philosophical Enquiry Into the Origin of Our Ideas of the Sublime and Beautiful,* ed. with introduction and notes by J. T. Boulton (New York: Columbia University Press, 1958), p. xxv.

28. Ayling, *Edmund Burke,* pp. 154-55.

29. Ibid., p. 13.

30. Thomas Copeland, *Our Eminent Friend Edmund Burke* (New Haven, CT: Yale University Press, 1949), p. 143.

31. "An Essay Towards an Abridgement of the English History," *Works,* VII, pp. 157-488.

32. A modern edition of the volumes on America actually appears with Edmund Burke's name rather than William's; *An Account of the European Settlements in America,* vols. 1 & 2 (New York: Arno, 1972).

33. Thomas H. D. Mahoney, *Edmund Burke and Ireland* (Cambridge, MA: Harvard University Press, 1960), p. 10.

34. Quoted in Carl B. Cone, *Burke and the Nature of Politics: The Age of the American Revolution* (Lexington: University of Kentucky Press, 1957), pp. 69-70.

35. One of the main themes of O'Brien's recent biography is that for Burke, because of his suspect Catholic upbringing, "habitual reticence was the norm, and dissimulation an occasional resource." O'Brien, *The Great Melody,* p. 13.

36. See the chapter on the "bluestockings" in Donald C. Bryant, *Edmund Burke and His Literary Friends* (St. Louis., MO: Washington University Studies, 1939).

37. *Corr.,* IV, p. 228. Burke had also aligned himself to some degree with extraparliamentary politics in the "county movement" in 1779, at least insofar as it was aimed toward promoting administrative reforms that might cut down the power of the Crown; see O'Brien, *The Great Melody,* pp. 209-13. Apparently Burke later deeply regretted his having "given way to popularity" in this instance." *Corr.,* IX, p. 274.

38. "Speech to the Electors of Bristol," November 1774, *Works,* II, pp. 88-98.

39. *Corr.,* IV, pp. 268-69, 295.

40. Roy Porter, *English Society in the Eighteenth Century* (London: Penguin, 1982) p. 116.

41. *Corr.,* IV, p. 246.

42. O'Brien, *The Great Melody,* p. 77.

43. "Speech on a Bill for Shortening the Duration of Parliaments, May 8, 1780," *Works,* VII, p. 78.

44. Cf. "Speech on . . . Economical Reformation," *Works,* II, p. 359.

45. Prefatory letter to "Observations on the Conduct of the Minority," *WS,* VIII, p. 404. Conor Cruise O'Brien has also assigned the Gordon Riots a significant role in Burke's life and thought. His position, however, is somewhat different from mine. For him, the monster that most haunted Burke was that of a heated, tyrannical mode of anti-Catholic politics that could burst from beneath the traditional mode of oppressive British rule over Catholics in Ireland and England. In the Gordon Riots, Burke saw this "dragon" in its most immediate and frightening form. According to this interpretation, what linked the riots of 1780 with the French Revolution was the anti-Catholic dimension. O'Brien, *The Great Melody,* pp. 77-86, 394-96. I think there is probably some truth in O'Brien's interpretation. However, if one takes it as the whole truth of Burke's mind, one is much harder pressed to comprehend the *specific* depth, character, and intensity of Burke's engagement with the French Revolution. O'Brien, in effect, largely demotes this event to one more instance of anti-Catholicism. I want to stress on the contrary that Burke saw something radically new on the historical horizon. And he looked back at the Gordon Riots as one of the first signs of this novel phenomenon. In relation to O'Brien's claim that the Irish Catholic "layer" of Burke's psyche is the key to all his thoughts and struggles, one might consider the judgment of the editor of the recent volume of *Writings and Speeches* that includes the materials on Ireland. R. B. McDowell writes: "An Irishman settled in England, Burke showed no signs of being disturbed by inner tensions caused by conscious or subconscious efforts at reconciling two different cultural traditions. If there were distinct national characteristics, they were for him of minor significance compared to the common literary and political heritage, the way of life, and the friendships shared by men of education, property, and enterprise in both countries"; *WS,* IX, p. 394.

46. "Observations on the Conduct," *WS,* VIII, p. 406.

47. "Fourth Letter on a Regicide Peace," *WS,* IX, pp. 83-84.

48. "Letter to a Noble Lord" (1796), *Works,* V, p. 181.

49. *Corr.,* V, pp. xviii, 295.

50. L. G. Mitchell, "Introduction," *WS,* VIII, p. 29.

51. "Speech on Opening of Impeachment," *WS,* VI, p. 275.

52. *Corr.,* VII, p. 553.

53. *Corr.,* VIII, p. 254.

54. Kramnick, *The Rage of Edmund Burke,* p. xii. J. G. A. Pocock rightly cautions against portrayals of eighteenth-century English society as composed of a coherent bourgeois class confronting a coherent aristocracy; see "The Varieties of Whiggism from Exclusion to Reform," in *Virtue, Commerce, and History: Essays on Political Thought and History, Chiefly in the Eighteenth Century* (Cambridge: Cambridge University Press, 1982), pp. 261-62; also his "Introduction" in Edmund Burke, *Reflections on the Revolution in France* (New York: Hackett, 1987).

55. Burke uses the term "political architect" in "Speech on the State of Representation" (1782), *Works,* VII, p. 91.

56. "Appeal From the New to the Old Whigs," *Works,* IV, pp. 57-215.

57. *WS,* IX.

58. *Corr.,* VIII, p. 129.

2

The Sublime, the Beautiful, and the Political

The house of Burke's close friend, Samuel Johnson, is preserved today as a small museum tucked away on a side street in the center of London. Among the many objects relating to Johnson's life and times is a portrait of Burke. The explanatory note below the picture informs us that the subject of the painting was "once known for his *political* thought, now known primarily for his *A Philosophical Inquiry Into the Origins of Our Ideas of the Sublime and the Beautiful.*"[1] For anyone familiar with the history of political thought such a judgment comes as something of a shock. A similar, if milder, jolt results from opening a recent collection of essays celebrating the bicentennial of the *Reflections* and discovering that all of the contributors come from literature departments.[2]

What should political theorists make of such things? Perhaps there are some lessons to be learned, the most prominent of which may be that political theorists can no longer afford to think that the aesthetic or literary aspects of a major figure's work are something that can be safely set to one side while "serious" analysis is done. But the rise of the "literary" Burke may also teach us something about the relative poverty of political reflection on Burke during the cold war. On the right, Burke was too often reduced to a Christian crusader against anything that carried even a whiff of radicalism. Those on the left either tended to ignore him as not even worth confronting or sought to show that his motives were less saintly than the conservatives implied.[3] This cold war-Burke was, however, ultimately a pretty monochromic version of a richly-hued character.

If these "lessons" about Burke have any validity, then it makes some sense for political theorists to look much more carefully at the interconnection of Burke's aesthetic ideas and political views. This process has actually gotten well under way over the last few years; I hope simply to carry it forward in a somewhat more comprehensive and sustained fashion.[4]

I start with a discussion of the historical and intellectual origins of the *Inquiry* (Part I). Then the basic distinction between the beautiful and the sublime is analyzed, as well as how that distinction is interrelated with others, especially male/female and public/private (Part II). Finally, I trace how all of this is integrated with Burke's notion of judgment and his differentiation between "first" and "second nature" (Part III).

I. Origins of the *Inquiry*

Although the *Inquiry* is concerned with both the sublime and the beautiful, it becomes immediately apparent to the reader that it is the former topic that really holds Burke's interest. The word "sublime," according to the *Oxford English Dictionary,* seems to have been in general circulation in the early eighteenth century, usually being associated with things exalted, elevated, or rare. And it already appears to have been appropriated in popular culture in a way not dissimilar to mass media uses today, at least if we are to judge by the name of a men's club founded in 1735: "The Sublime Society of Beefsteaks."[5] Scholarly attention to the sublime began after *Peri Hupsous,* written by the first-century Greek writer Longinus, was translated in 1698 as *On the Sublime.*[6] Longinus was the standard authority when Burke turned to the topic in the 1740s and 1750s. But Burke was hardly the only Briton of his time to become fascinated with the sublime. The precise reason for this vogue is, of course, not easy to decipher with any certainty. Perhaps the fascination with a kind of deep and intense experience on the part of the educated elite of this era is not really too surprising. After all, from the Glorious Revolution of 1688 until the last

quarter of the eighteenth century, England experienced a period of relative
internal peace as well as a decline in the intensity of religious belief (both
among Protestant dissenters and in the Church of England). This does not
of course mean that the English no longer generally believed in God or
engaged in political struggle. What it does mean, however, is first, that
there existed no political zeal comparable either to that surrounding the
two revolutions in the seventeenth century or the last quarter of the eighteenth,
when modern revolutionary ideologies blossomed; and second, there existed no religious zeal comparable to that of the Puritans and others in the
seventeenth century.[7] If this is true, then the rise of attentiveness to an
aesthetic experience that seemed to partake of the thrill of epic political
deeds and the profundity of religious conviction becomes perhaps a little
more comprehensible.[8]

Peri Hupsous was required reading at Trinity College when Burke was
an undergraduate in the 1740s. And it was during his undergraduate years
that he began to work on what was to emerge in 1757 as the *Inquiry.*[9] Thus,
it is useful to glance briefly at Longinus's text to get some sense of what
Burke thought he was up to in his own work.

In *Peri Hupsous* the topic of the sublime is taken up as an issue in rhetoric. Sublimity is "a kind of height and conspicuous excellence in speeches
and writings"; and Longinus's intention is to help "men in political life"
attain it.[10] But such height and excellence are not attainable by just any
political hack who masters a set of techniques. One can indeed cultivate
techniques, yet at bottom the sublime is unalterably connected with "the
resonance of greatness of mind," whether that greatness be in a poet like
Homer or a political orator like Demosthenes. What constitutes such greatness or nobility, at least in regard to sublimity, is a sensibility engaged with
the problem of human limits. This engagement is twofold. On the one hand,
sublimity is tied to the "thrust of human theorizing and perceptiveness,"
the passion to go "beyond the limits" of the ordinary, either in poetic expression or political action. On the other hand, this passion for *limitlessness* remains in tension with human *limitedness,* the parameters of which
form when we "gaze up openly at the cosmos" and when we reflect upon
the "hard destiny" or fate that awaits human projects.[11]

Longinus was not the only author interested in rhetoric that Burke stud-
ied. The curriculum at Trinity was heavily weighted toward this subject.[12]
Moreover, Burke was an avid member of a college club that continually

held debates on a variety of subjects. There is no doubt that this early experience had an effect on how Burke constructed his later political writings and indeed his very identity as a political actor. Philip Francis, with whom Burke worked closely during the effort to impeach Hastings, even suggested that his friend consciously modeled his career on that of Cicero.[13]

Given this early emphasis on rhetoric and the later choice of career, it is rather surprising to discover that the *Inquiry* says very little about oratory or public life. The last and shortest of the five parts of the book is about how words affect the passions and imagination. This is, of course, applicable to political speech, but Burke speaks almost exclusively about poetry. His examples here, as elsewhere in the text, are drawn more from figures such as Homer or Milton than from Demosthenes or Cicero. Similarly, he says hardly anything explicitly about Longinus. Rather Burke is concerned primarily with the task of providing a new way of understanding the distinction between the beautiful and the sublime, one grounded in a sensationist account of the human mind. His views here run directly counter to one of the leading philosophers of this era, Francis Hutcheson. Hutcheson's *Inquiry Into the Original of Our Ideas of Beauty and Virtue* (1725) suggests that we have a special "internal sense" or faculty that allows us to be pleased by objects of beauty. Hutcheson follows the classical notion that beauty is found in objects exhibiting "Regularity, Order, Harmony." This mode of being affected extends also to the sphere of morality; we are pleased by "Virtue, or the Beauty of Action."[14]

Perhaps Burke chose the title of his book to draw attention to the contrasts between Hutcheson's views and his own. Unlike his predecessor, Burke elevates the sublime to an independent status within aesthetics; moreover, he does not offer a systematic account of the connection of aesthetics and morality. To a large degree, Burke appears in his text as an empirical psychologist exploring what one might call the natural economy of the passions and imagination; in other words, how certain objects, by their "natural powers," cause—either directly or through the mediation of the imagination—corresponding passions to occur.[15] He has no patience for Hutcheson's postulation of special "internal" senses.

The picture of Burke doing critical or "scientific" analysis and Hutcheson doing speculative philosophy on the boundary of aesthetics and morality is correct to a degree. At least in intention, much of the *Inquiry* reads like an empirical and analytical treatment of the aesthetic-affective domain that is, as it were, "beyond good and evil." No moral doctrine is immediately at issue. It would be a serious mistake, though, to take this as an adequate picture of what is going on in the *Inquiry.* The natural economy of passions and imagination that Burke sketches is ultimately grounded in God's purposes. As he says elsewhere, we do not have "Passions which have no Purpose."[16] But Burke gives no extensive arguments for this claim in the *Inquiry.* Indeed, where he does make the claim explicitly, it sounds—at least to contemporary ears—a bit like a simple add-on gesture of conciliation toward readers with strong religious beliefs. All this might lead one to think that Burke did not take such remarks very seriously.[17] The contrary, however, is the case.

This question is no minor one. In fact, it embodies a set of issues that run through Burke's writings as a whole and divide his interpreters. On the one hand, it is difficult to confront Burke's writings and letters without gaining the sense that his view of the world is deeply imbued with religious feeling. The power of this feeling is, I would suggest, what provides initial plausibility to the interpretation of Burke as essentially a proponent of "the classical and Scholastic moral Natural Law."[18] But this interpretation is ultimately pretty unsatisfying. It has been argued rather persuasively that Burke's notion of natural law was a conventional, partially Lockean version that had a convincing ring for the political elites he was primarily concerned to persuade.[19] Acceptance of this argument does not mean, however, that one must as a consequence see Burke simply using religion for purely rhetorical purposes. Rather, it merely means that attempts to understand the distinctiveness of Burke's thought are not going to be enhanced by initially viewing him as a natural law thinker.

There is a further important reason to resist the effort to reduce Burke's thought to natural law dimensions.[20] Within the natural law tradition, God's relation to the world is understood as stable and unchanging. His intentions are inscribed in an fixed natural order. Burke certainly believes in the idea of a great chain of being, a God-ordained moral order. But there is a sense in which this order cannot be taken as absolutely certain. The relation of Burke's God to the world, that is, Providence, is uncertain. In the year before his death, Burke expresses this sentiment succinctly. Deeply pessimistic about Britain's likelihood of resisting the tide of revolution, he begins his "First Letter on a Regicide Peace" with a reference to "the awful drama of Providence, now acting on the moral theatre of the world."[21] The drama of human life ultimately does not follow a knowable script, but rather unfolds according to the mysterious will of its divine director.[22] It is because Burke believes this that even when he is adamantly attacking the French Revolution, he worries that perhaps he is fighting not just human adversaries but Providence itself. He cannot be absolutely certain that the light of nature ever shines with perfect clarity. At the very end of "Thoughts on French Affairs," in 1791, Burke betrays his deep anxiety:

> This subject . . . has given me many anxious moments for the two last years. If a great change is to be made in human affairs, the minds of men will be fitted to it; the general opinions and feelings will draw that way. Every fear, every hope, will forward it; and then they who persist in opposing this mighty current in human affairs, will appear rather to resist the decrees of Providence itself, than the mere designs of men. They will not be resolute and firm, but perverse and obstinate.[23]

Similarly, five years later Burke confides to a French emigré, Abbé de La Bintinaye: "It seems as if it were God's will, that the present order of things is to be destroyed; and that it is vain to struggle with that dispensation."[24]

I want to suggest that we should indeed take the religious dimension of Burke's thinking seriously, but that we must understand it somewhat differently from those who wish to enlist him in the ranks of the natural law corps. If we do this, we will get a better sense of where the power lies in Burke's critique of modernity, as well as where it falls flat. In general, I want to show that it is Burke's entwinement of aesthetics with his persistent attention to human finitude that provides him with his insights into the dangers of modern politics. The seeds of this perspective are planted in the *Inquiry,* more specifically in the way he construes the sublime.

II. Distinguishing the Sublime From the Beautiful

Before Burke, discussions of aesthetics typically attended primarily to the qualities an object or phenomenon must have to be considered sublime or beautiful. Burke is certainly interested in this aspect, as I will show in a moment, but his analysis is unusual for the attention he pays to analyzing the subjective experience of sublimity and beauty.[25] In effect, he wants to map out those domains of the human passions which come into play when an individual is confronted with an aesthetic object. Like many eighteenth-century philosophers, Burke begins his analysis by arranging the passions generally around two basic purposes: "self-preservation, and *society*."[26] The passions of self-preservation relate to our character as fragile, vulnerable, mortal creatures; and the passions of society relate to our character as creatures who must reproduce, and who seek friendship and human contact in general. The former passions fall into the domain of pain and the latter into that of pleasure.

That which is beautiful clearly causes pleasure; but what about the sublime? Burke places it squarely in the camp of pain. And yet there is, of course, a sort of pleasure involved with the sublime. Burke explains this phenomenon as follows. A sublime experience is one evoked by something that confronts us with our vulnerability and is thus painful; however, the threat in this case remains at a distance. It is this distance that gives us the cognitive and emotional space necessary for sublimity. If the threat is too close or immediate, we simply experience the pain of being terrified and disoriented. Burke uses the word "delight" to name this peculiar pleasure shadowed by human fragility.[27] The particular passions associated with this delight are typically "astonishment," "awe, reverence, and respect." Objects of beauty, on the other hand, are associated with the passions of "love" and "affection and tenderness."[28]

Burke's mapping of the passions is joined with an attempt to show the actual physiological mechanism by which causation takes place. This effort gives rise to some of the more amusing sections of the essay, as when the author tries to show how the experience of sublimity is rooted in "an unnatural tension of the nerves." The comic high point is reached when he informs us that "beauty acts by relaxing the solids" of the nervous system.[29] With a cool "scientific" eye, Burke describes to the (male) reader the physiological effects of being confronted with beauty:

> The head reclines something on one side; the eyelids are more closed than usual, and the eyes roll gently with an inclination to the object; the mouth is a little opened, and the breath drawn slowly, with now and then a low sigh; the whole body is composed, and the hands fall idly to the sides. All this is accompanied with an inward sense of melting and languor. These appearances are always proportioned to the degree of beauty in the object, and of sensibility in the observer. And this graduation from the highest pitch of beauty and sensibility, even to the lowest of mediocrity and indifference, and their

correspondent effects, ought to be kept in view, else this description will seem exaggerated, which it certainly is not.[30]

This sentimentalized portrait of beauty did not sit particularly well with early reviewers of the *Inquiry,* who were used to the classical picture of beauty that associated it with qualities such as fitness, proportionality, regularity, and the like. The portrait of the sublime also struck Burke's contemporaries as somewhat odd. Especially unsettling was the claim that the sublime was essentially connected with horror or terror. Burke reasoned that pain is always tied to what is fearful or terrifying; and as the sublime is at least partially rooted in a painful experience, then it must necessarily also be tied to what is fearful or horrible.[31]

This way of refiguring the sublime shifts it somewhat away from its familiar Longinian association with the limitlessness of the heroic and the "resonance of greatness of mind." One of Burke's critics, writing shortly after his death, tried to illustrate the absurdity of this novel move with the following example. If Burke, he imagined,

> had walked up St. James street without his breeches, it would have occasioned great and universal *astonishment;* and if he had, at the same time, carried a loaded blunderbuss in his hands, the astonishment would have been mixed with no small portion of *terror:* but I do not believe the united effects of these two powerful passions would have produced any sentiment or sensation approaching to sublime.[32]

This critic, although admiring Burke, lamented the influence his emphasis on terror and the sublime had had on British taste in the second half of the eighteenth century. Burke's followers seemed to feel he had given them license to create works "which teem with all sorts of terrific and horrific monsters and hobgoblins."[33]

When Burke brought out a second edition of the *Inquiry* in 1759, he made various modifications in the text.[34] The most significant of these relate to the sublime and terror. What is striking is that none of the changes mute in any way his initial claim; rather they amplify and elucidate it. Burke's stand is crystal clear: "Terror is in all cases, either more openly or latently, the ruling principle of the sublime."[35] The question that arises rather quickly is why did Burke persist in this refiguring of the sublime, given the Longinian tradition and the apparently apt criticism of his reviewers?

This persistence ultimately has to do with the particular religious sense of Burke's thinking. To explain exactly what I mean by this, it is necessary to say a bit more about this sense. To a large degree, he shared with many Anglicans of his time a perspective known as "latitudinarianism." This was generally associated with tolerance on matters of Christian doctrine, as well as a willingness to see reason and natural religion as important sources of Christian truth, along with revelation. This sort of position is compatible with the one Burke adopts in his *Vindication of Natural Society.* There Burke parodies Bolingbroke's view that revelation is superfluous, because reason and natural religion are *all* we need. This text has some-times been read as implying that Burke completely rejects the value of reason and natural religion. But that interpretation overstates things.[36] Burke is very much interested, as I indicated earlier, in how the natural economy of the passions and imagination are connected to God's purposes. This appears to be a crucial part of the picture he sees himself drawing in the *Inquiry.*[37]

In his distinctive refiguring of the sublime Burke is telling us that its deepest significance as a category of human experience resides in the way it confronts us with our finitude. This is the heart of what Burke is getting at in his insistence that the sublime is associated with terror; for as he says, death is the "*king of terrors,*" and all pain is merely its "*emissary.*"[38] What gives the concept of the sublime its coherence then is its reference to a natural, experiential basis for a reflective confrontation with death; a con-frontation that is neither merely a cognitive pondering nor an emotional reaction, but rather an experience in which cognition and passion are in-extricably bound up with one another.

Not every sublime experience, of course, has to threaten one literally with death or severe pain. Sublimity admits of degrees. These are related to the intensity with which the limitedness of human being is vivified. Darkness may evoke it, as the loss of light removes the confidence that comes with having a known context. Similarly, it can be very lightly evoked, Burke says, when one looks down a long row of uniform columns, because the eye is forced to cast its glance along a path that seems to exceed its possible visual field.[39] Finally, from within this framework, one can now see how a response might be crafted to the apparently devastating critical example referred to above. Although the critic wished to trade on the comical or absurd quality of the image of a demented Burke stalking the streets, one might suggest that this is only part of what might be one's reaction. Amusement with the absurdity of such a scene might very well be haunted with an anxiety arising from a confrontation with madness. What greater living threat is there to our ability to construct and maintain our boundaries of self and world?

While Burke was at Trinity and beginning to form the project of the *Inquiry,* he wrote a letter to a very close friend that sheds light on the way he came to refigure the sublime. Burke lived in a section of Dublin that flooded from time to time. In the letter he describes his mood during a flood that was far worse than any he had previously experienced. Because the water rose slowly, the threat of death was imminent, but not immediate. This afforded him time to reflect and gave his mood that peculiarly ambivalent quality: fear mixed with a strange pleasure.

> No one perhaps has seen such a flood here as we have now. . . . All our Cellars are drowned not as before for that was but a trifle to this, for now the water comes up to the first floor of the House threatening us every minute with rising a great deal higher[,] the Consequence of which would infallibly be the fall of the house.

> It gives me pleasure to see nature in those great tho' terrible Scenes, it fills the mind with grand ideas, and turns the Soul in upon herself. This . . . forced some reflections on me. . . . I considered how little man is yet in his own mind how great![40]

If my interpretation of Burke's sublime is correct, then it helps one to understand the strong emphasis (noted in Chapter 1) he places throughout his life on the importance of humility as a source of both wisdom and virtue. From the confrontation with finitude or limitedness, there should arise a strong sense of humility that in turn ought to animate all our actions.

Contrast this now with Longinus. There one finds much greater emphasis on the sublime's relation to the *limitless* "thrusting" of human will and intelligence, even if it is ultimately played out against a background of "hard destiny." In Burke, on the contrary, it is human *limitedness* that is emphasized. This does not mean that he explicitly condemns, say, Homeric heroes or a figure like Demosthenes, who plays such a large role in Longinus. Nor does it mean that he condemns ambition in general.[41] What it does

mean though is that Burke's notion of the sublime prepares him to be acutely
sensitive to the novelty of the aesthetic-affective dynamics displayed in
the revolutionary consciousness that emerges full blown in the French
Revolution. Many things about that revolution horrified Burke, but nothing more than his sense that it announced a new, modern world that would
unfold itself in the medium of a "false sublime": one that annihilates the
confrontation with finitude. If Burke had remained more conventional in
his understanding of the sublime, his critique might not have had this dimension. For after all, the French revolutionaries worked hard at clothing
themselves in the paraphernalia of the heroes and glory of republican Rome.
In a sense, they consciously cultivated an image of themselves as classi-
cally sublime. Burke, however, saw something radically different going on.

Burke envisions the distinction between the sublime and the beautiful
as being naturally aligned with two other distinctions: public and private,
and male and female. These distinctions are in turn aligned with Burke's
lifelong belief that all existence is linked in a great chain of superiors and
subordinates.[42] Wherever there is superiority and power, there is the potential to harm others, either physically or through adverse judgment. Thus,
there is naturally some feeling of the sublime when those who are inferior
in position "look up," as it were, at their superiors. Superior position is also
naturally associated with "great virtues" such as "fortitude, justice, wisdom and the like."[43] This aesthetic-affective dynamic holds true both in
the "public" relations of leaders and people, and in the "private" relations
of men and women.

Burke does not actually say much explicitly about politics in the *Inquiry.*
Rather his discussion revolves heavily around the "private" sphere of gender,
particularly when he is showing how the beautiful is distinguished from
the sublime. Objects of beauty, as we have seen, are ones that evoke not
awe or respect, but "love" and "affection and tenderness." The physical
qualities that excite these passions are diminutive size, smoothness, deli-
cateness or fragility, and weakness; in short, all the sorts of qualities Burke
associated with beauty in women. Objects of beauty thus seem inextricably tied to a degree of inferiority or imperfection (a point Burke wishes to
stress to undermine the classical view of beauty as consisting in perfec-
tion). The virtues or "qualities of mind" that naturally complement these
physical qualities are the "lesser" or "softer," "domestic" ones, such as "easi-
ness of temper, compassion, kindness and liberality."[44]

It is abundantly clear from this chain of argument that in Burke's view there is a strong natural symmetry between aesthetics, gender, and power. This symmetry admits of some exceptions, however. For example, he does allow the beautiful to have a place in relationships between men. Here physical qualities are not at issue, only the "qualities of mind." The bond of affection in male friendship is thus to be explained as constituted out of the mutual expression and appreciation of the "domestic" virtues.[45]

Another variation on the natural symmetry of aesthetics, gender, and power emerges within the family. Burke offers a curious illustration of how aesthetic-affective dynamics work across generations:

> The authority of a father, so useful to our well-being, and so justly venerable upon all accounts, hinders us from having the entire love for him that we have for our mothers, where the parental authority is almost melted down into the mother's fondness and indulgence. But we generally have a great love for our grandfathers, in whom this authority is removed a degree from us, and where the weakness of age mellows it into something of a feminine partiality.[46]

This example is not particularly important for Burke in 1757. It becomes quite significant later on, however, although the reason for this will only become apparent in the next chapter, when I connect it with the way Burke began to conceive of authority and tradition in the 1780s.

III. Nature and Judgment

In the first edition of the *Inquiry,* Burke is generally quite adamant that the economy of our aesthetic-affective life is a natural one. Certain objects or phenomena call forth corresponding passions simply by virtue of their "natural powers." Burke does admit that some things affect us by "associated," rather than by natural, powers, but he suspects that such association can somehow be traced back to a natural source. In any case, he concludes, it would be "to little purpose to look for the cause of our passions in association, until we fail of it in the natural properties of things."[47]

In the second edition, Burke seems to allow that our aesthetic-affective life may be rather more deeply influenced by association. Natural reactions may be radically modified by long association. Habit or custom, for example, may make someone prefer the bitter taste of tobacco to the sweet taste of sugar, even though sweet things naturally give us more pleasure. Such "acquired relish" constitutes a kind of "second nature." Burke continues to maintain, however, that we can still separate out our "first" nature and understand its distinct reactions. In short, there is still the possibility of a universally valid knowledge regarding "natural pleasures and pains."[48] Whatever one may think about this argument in regard to taste in a narrow sense (regarding sugar, for example), one cannot help feeling that in regard to taste in the broader sense of aesthetics and morality Burke is not very convincing. The case is left more at the level of assertion than persuasion. He simply is unable to entertain the possibility that second nature goes "all the way down." For to admit that would be to cast the economy of the passions and imagination adrift from its anchorage in divine purposes. That possibility was something of a nightmare image for Burke, especially as he believed that our reason is far less effective in controlling our passions than we tend to think.[49]

Just as the importance of the sphere of association expands in the second edition, so also does that of judgment. The natural economy of the passions and imagination in the first edition is, as I have noted, almost independent of morality. Presumably Burke felt that his grounding of that economy in God's purposes was all that was needed. In the second edition, however, he adds an introductory essay "On Taste," in which he tries to make clear that aesthetic-affective response is at least partially superintended by critical judgment. If the object of experience involves "the manners, the characters, the actions, and designs of men, their relations, their virtues and vices, they come within the province of judgment."[50]

We may respond to such phenomena (either as they present themselves directly or through works of art) by finding them beautiful or sublime; that is, we may, for example, find someone's character to be beautiful or an action to be sublime. But our response may in fact be "wrong," in the sense that it shows a lack of good judgment or taste. And good judgment depends not just upon natural "sensibility," but also upon the degree of one's experience and the carefulness of one's reasoning.[51]

Burke thus gives to judgment a fairly substantial judicial function: "The judgment is for the greater part employed in throwing stumbling blocks in the way of the imagination, in dissipating the scenes of its enchantment, and in tying us down to the disagreeable yoke of our reason."[52] In the first edition, Burke indicated that it made little sense to say that one "ought" or "ought not" to find something beautiful or sublime.[53] Yet that seems precisely the sort of judgment he is creating a justification for in the second edition. And it is just this sort of moral-aesthetic judgment that he later brings to bear on political life.

If the expanded role of moral-aesthetic judgment in the final version of the *Inquiry* is crucial for Burke's later political ideas, so also is his expansion of the place of "second" nature; that is, nature as formed by custom and tradition. Its prominence is what gives Burke's thought a remarkable suppleness when it comes to considering political arrangements in different circumstances. The necessity of doing justice to "second nature" is what makes politics such a complex art and "prudence" such an important virtue. Political leaders must not only ask themselves how some policy or institution will suit man's "first" nature, but also "does it suit his nature as modified by his habits?"[54]

Burke nevertheless always retained, as noted above, his faith that there was a "first" or primary universal human nature, even though most of his actual insights about politics do not result from an employment of it. In effect, the appeal to nature in the abstract is certain, but its guidance for judgment in concrete circumstances is deeply uncertain, or at least it is for most of Burke's parliamentary career. By "uncertainty" here I do not mean a lack of decisiveness on Burke's part, but rather an initial flexibility, an openness to alternative opinions, a willingness to seek compromise when apparently legitimate principles were in conflict, and an extraordinary sense of obligation to inform himself thoroughly on the particulars of a situation. These qualities of his thought express his sense of how extensively second nature constitutes the stuff of political life.

Later, when Burke confronts political modernity head on, his thought becomes far more rigid. "First" nature comes into its own as the criterion for attacking the evils of "Indianism and Jacobinism" with the certainty worthy of a crusader. For Burke these are *unnatural* perversions, and there is no lack of certainty in his recommendations to crush them in every one of their concrete manifestations.

But there is something unsettling about these absolutist judgments apparently grounded in knowledge of "first" nature. If, as was shown earlier,

Burke viewed Providence as dramatic, mysterious, and unpredictable, then the certainty of many of his specific judgments sits poorly with his own deepest convictions. Consider in this light the Hastings trial. Was Burke really warranted in his demonization of Hastings as the "captain general in iniquity"? Hastings no doubt did some reprehensible things.[55] But Burke compartmentalized his judgments here in a fashion that is far from acceptable. The demonization of Hastings stands in sharp contrast to Burke's unwillingness to raise broader questions about the overall legitimacy of Great Britain's domination of India. Providence, which for Burke was usually shrouded in mystery, is here seen as having made its decrees crystal clear. The "dominion of the glorious Empire" is, he confidently announces, "given by an incomprehensible dispensation of the Divine providence into our hands."[56] This is hardly Burke at his best. He would have shredded such an argument to pieces if it had been used against him in regard to another political issue. For example, he had no difficulty taking the stance that the institution of slavery and the slave trade of Africans in the western hemisphere could and should be completely dismantled.[57]

The same blind imbalance of judgment infected his pronouncements about the French Revolution, as generations of commentators have asserted from Burke's day to the present. For example, in his desire to portray the French as unnatural monsters, he seized upon false and sensationalized newspaper reports of cannibalism to justify the blanket epithet of "Cannibal Republic."[58] Such language cannot be dismissed as mere hyperbole. Burke's absolute refusal to consider any negotiated peace with the French was directly tied to the extremity of his judgment of the revolutionaries as evil incarnate. Nothing short of total "extinction" of every vestige of the revolution would do for him.[59] A full-scale invasion of France had to be launched; and he warned that none of the invading force should know the French language.[60] One could not have the devil whispering in the ears of British soldiers.

Burke's interpreters often speak of his writings as containing not so much a theory as a body of political wisdom. This is a fair observation. But it strains the term "wisdom" to apply it to the kinds of judgments I have just noted. If this is so, how might we begin to separate the core of that wisdom from specific judgments that did not do justice to it? We can do this, I believe, if we attend to Burke's understanding of the sublime and the way it progressively structures his reactions to political modernity across the span of his career.

Notes

1. My emphasis.

2. Steven Blakemore, ed., *Burke and the French Revolution: Bicentennial Essays* (Athens: University of Georgia Press, 1992).

3. For political reflection on the right, see especially Russell Kirk, *The Conservative Mind* (Chicago: Regnery, 1953), Chap. 1-2, 13; and Peter Stanlis, *Edmund Burke and the Natural Law* (Ann Arbor: University of Michigan Press, 1958). On the left, see C. B. Macpherson, *Burke* (New York: Hill & Wang, 1980); and Sheldon Wolin, *Politics and Vision* (Boston: Little, Brown, 1960), in which there is only a passing reference to Burke. Inattention by the left may have resulted from an attitude succinctly expressed by Raymond Williams: "The confutation of Burke on the French Revolution is now a one-finger exercise in politics and history"; *Culture and Society, 1780-1950* (London: Pelican, 1961), p. 24.

4. Political theorists who have paid some attention to the aesthetic dimension in Burke are Neal Wood, "The Aesthetic Dimension in Burke's Political Thought," *Journal of British Studies* 4 (1964): 41-64; B. T. Wilkins, *The Problem of Burke's Political Philosophy* (Oxford, U.K.: Clarendon, 1967), pp. 119-51; Isaac Kramnick, *The Rage of Edmund Burke: Portrait of an Ambivalent Conservative* (New York: Basic Books, 1977); Bruce James Smith, *Politics and Remembrance: Republican Themes in Machiavelli, Burke and Tocqueville* (Princeton, NJ: Princeton University Press, 1985), Chap. 3; William Corlett, *Community Without Unity: A Politics of Derridian Extravagance* (Durham, NC, & London: Duke University Press, 1989), Chap. 6; and Ian Hampshire-Monk, "Rhetoric and Opinion in the Politics of Edmund Burke," *History of Political Thought* 9, 3 (Winter 1988): 467ff. A recent and very interesting book-length addition to the literature on Burke's aesthetic dimension is Paul Hindson and Tim Gray, *Burke's Dramatic Theory of Politics* (Aldershot, U.K.: Avebury, 1988).

5. Roy Porter, *English Society in the Eighteenth Century* (London: Penguin, 1982), p. 172.

6. J. T. Boulton, "Editor's Introduction" in Edmund Burke, *A Philosophical Enquiry Into the Origin of Our Ideas of the Sublime and Beautiful,* ed. with introduction and notes by J. T. Boulton (New York: Columbia University Press, 1958), pp. xvi, xlivff.

7. On the decline in the intensity of religious faith, see Porter, *English Society in the Eighteenth Century,* pp. 184-200.

8. Cf. Frans De Bruyn, "Hooking the Leviathan: The Eclipse of the Heroic and the Emergence of the Sublime in Eighteenth Century British Literature," *The Eighteenth Century: Theory and Interpretation* 28, 1 (Winter 1987): 195-215; and Thomas Weiskel, *The Romantic Sublime: Studies in the Structure and Psychology of Transcendence* (Baltimore, MD: Johns Hopkins University Press, 1976), p. 3.

9. "Introduction," p. xvi.

10. Longinus, *On the Sublime,* trans. with commentary by James A. Arieti & John M. Crossett (New York: Edwin Mellen, 1985), pp. 6-9.

11. Ibid., pp. 52-3, 56, 177, 229.

12. Ian Hampsher-Monk, "Rhetoric and Opinion in the Politics of Edmund Burke," pp. 458-59.

13. Ibid.

14. Francis Hutcheson, *An Inquiry Into the Original of Our Ideas of Beauty and Virtue* (London: J. Darby, 1726; reprinted New York: Garland, 1971), pp. xiv-xv, 106.

15. Ibid., pp. 179-80, 209-10. Burke does not refer to Hutcheson by name in the text of the *Inquiry,* but he does attack the idea of internal senses; *Inquiry,* pp. 98-99, 190.

16. *A Notebook of Edmund Burke,* ed. H. V. F. Somerset (Cambridge: Cambridge University Press, 1957), p. 71; and *Inquiry, Works,* I, pp. 113, 119, 126-127.

17. The religious dimension of Burke's thinking is totally ignored by the editor of a recent edition of the *Inquiry.* Adam Phillips writes: "In Burke's *Enquiry,* with its relatively cursory references to Christianity, we find the beginnings of a . . . new erotic empiricism"; Phillips's "Introduction" in Edmund Burke, *A Philosophical Enquiry into the Origin of our Ideas of the Sublime and the Beautiful* (Oxford: Oxford University Press, 1990) p. xi.

18. Peter Stanlis, *The Enlightenment and Revolution,* with a Foreword by Russell Kirk (New Brunswick, NJ: Transaction, 1991), p. 25.

19. See Frederick A. Dreyer, *Burke's Politics: A Study in Whig Orthodoxy* (Waterloo, Ontario: Wilfred Laurier University Press, 1979), pp. 80-81; and Frank O'Gorman, *Edmund Burke: His Political Philosophy* (Bloomington & London: Indiana University Press, 1973); pp. 98, 104-5. It is interesting to note also that one of the leading contemporary defenders of a Thomist position in political philosophy, Alisdair MacIntyre, summarily dismisses Burke as having nothing of value to say on the topic of natural law; see *Whose Justice, Which Rationality?* (Notre Dame, IN: University of Notre Dame Press, 1988), pp. 215-18, 228-31.

20. My account in this paragraph closely follows the insights of Hindson and Gray, *Burke's Dramatic Theory of Politics,* pp. 124-27.

21. "First Letter on a Regicide Peace," *WS,* IX, p. 188.

22. Hindson and Gray trace this conception of Providence in Burke back to his "An Essay Towards an Abridgement of the English History"; Hindson and Gray, *Burke's Dramatic Theory of Politics,* pp. 149ff.

23. "Thoughts on French Affairs," *WS,* VIII, p. 386.

24. *Corr.,* VIII, p. 412; cf. *Corr.,* IX, p. 307.

25. Samuel Monk, *The Sublime: A Study of Critical Theories in XVIII-Century England,* 2nd ed. (Ann Arbor: University of Michigan Press, 1950), pp. 4-5.

26. *Inquiry, Works,* I, p. 210.

27. Ibid., pp. 106-11.

28. Ibid., pp. 125, 130, 165, 216-17.

29. Ibid., pp. 211, 214, 218, 232-33.

30. Ibid., p. 232.

31. Ibid., pp. 130-31. On the response of Burke's early critics, see Herbert A. Wickelns, *Journal of English and Germanic Philology* 21, 4 (1922): 645-61; and Boulton, "Introduction."

32. Richard Payne Knight, *An Analytical Inquiry Into the Principles of Taste,* 2nd ed. (London: T. Payne, 1805), p. 377.

33. Ibid., p. 378.

34. The text typically available today, and the one reprinted in *Works,* is the second edition.

35. *Inquiry, Works,* I, p. 131.

36. On these questions of religion, see Frederick Dreyer, "Burke's Religion," *Studies in Burke and His Time,* 17, 3 (1976): 201ff.

37. A letter from a roommate of Burke's at Trinity, William Dennis, throws some light on this question. Dennis, who presumably discussed the basic ideas of the *Inquiry* with Burke, wrote a letter to a mutual friend in which he contrasted Hutcheson's work with Burke's. The former, he said, "indirectly saps religion by representing virtue independent of it"; the latter, on the other hand, "enlarges the understanding" in a way compatible with religion. The letter is quoted in Arthur P. I. Samuels, *The Early Life, Correspondence and Writings of the Rt. Honorable Edmund Burke* (Cambridge: Cambridge University Press, 1923), p. 212.

38. *Inquiry,* pp. 110-11. My emphasis.

39. Ibid., pp. 221-25.

40. *Corr.,* I, pp. 38-39.

41. See the section "Ambition" in the *Inquiry, Works* I, pp. 123-24.

42. *Inquiry, Works,* I, pp. 116, 210.

43. Ibid., pp. 188-89.

44. Ibid., pp. 125, 165, 188-89, 243.

45. Ibid., pp. 115-16.

46. Ibid., pp. 189-90.

47. Ibid., p. 210.

48. Ibid., pp. 83ff, 179-80, 209-10.

49. Ibid., p. 118.

50. Ibid., p. 94.

51. Ibid., pp. 94-95.

52. Ibid., p. 97.

53. Ibid., p. 188.

54. "Speech on Representation," *Works,* VII, pp. 96-98.

55. For a balanced judgment of the whole impeachment affair, see P. J. Marshall, *The Impeachment of Warren Hastings* (Oxford: Oxford University Press, 1965).

56. *Corr.,* IX, p. 62.

57. Burke did not advocate an immediate abolition of slavery; rather he favored systematically regulating it to death. He would certainly have summarily dismissed arguments for slavery based on claims about providential design. See "Sketch of a Negro Code," *Works,* VI, pp. 255-90.

58. "Third Letter on a Regicide Peace," *WS,* IX, pp. 322-23.

59. *Corr.,* VII, pp. 517-18.

60. *Corr.,* VI, p. 258.

3

Interpreting the Political World

As I suggested in Chapter 1, the Burke who stepped onto the stage of Parliament in 1765 was both well informed and self-confident. And the ideas he had elaborated in the *Inquiry* were an integral strand in the fabric of his intellect. In this chapter, I begin considering how those ideas structured the way Burke came to perceive the world of politics. In reference to this question, one critic has recently gone so far as to assert that Burke's "political writings in general . . . might be read as an attempt to work out the respective roles of the sublime and beautiful in politics."[1] This is probably something of an overstatement, at least if it is interpreted to mean that the language of aesthetics is *the* key language that unlocks the meaning of all of Burke's political reflections. But if it is interpreted as claiming that many of Burke's most distinctive insights are deeply structured by his understanding of aesthetic-affective dynamics, then it rings true.

Critics interested in the aesthetic or literary side of Burke have tended to focus their attention primarily on the *Inquiry* and *Reflections on the Revolution in France*.[2] More specifically, they use the former to help them understand the political insights contained in the latter. It is not difficult to understand the perennial attractiveness of this move. The *Reflections* is not only Burke's most well-known work, it is also a remarkably rich piece of literature on a number of grounds. I want to suggest, however, that this strategy entails a significant blindness. It assumes that the various things Burke wrote between these two works are of little or no importance in understanding the interplay of his aesthetic and political ideas. In this chapter, I will show such an assumption to be incorrect. The political writings of the "middle" period are crucially important. Only after one follows Burke's thinking through this period can one adequately understand the way in which his aesthetic theory structured his reflections on the French Revolution.

In order to set the stage for this analysis, I will first turn back to the *Inquiry* to elucidate how some of his brief remarks there on the interconnection of aesthetics, on the one hand, and social and political life, on the other, fit into broader currents of moral and political reflection in the early and middle eighteenth century (Part I). Then I will take up Burke's work between the *Inquiry* and the *Reflections*. This can be usefully divided into two segments, that before 1780 (Part II), and that between 1780 and 1790, the period in which he comes to understand political modernity in epochal terms (Part III).

I. The Problem of "Social Affection"

As I said in the last chapter, the *Inquiry* does not take up issues of politics in any systematic sense. But Burke does offer a few thoughts on the nature of social and political order. The sense of these thoughts really only becomes apparent, however, if one puts them in the context of some of the philosophical currents of his time. Once this sense is established, I will then show how it affects the way Burke construed political issues once he took up his public career.

A central problem for moral and political philosophers in the eighteenth century was understanding how passions related to the bonds of society. In one view, passions had primarily a negative connotation as unruly forces that threatened to pull society apart and that therefore had to be conquered. In another view, passions also had a positive connotation in the sense that they supported the bonds of social life.[3] Clearly, Burke is most fascinated by the latter view, as he maps out how the passions associated with beauty—love, tenderness, affection—serve the ends of "society." David Hume, among others, saw passions in this same general light, at least in his *Treatise of Human Nature* (1739-1740).[4] According to John Mullan, what Hume was trying to do there was to develop a "paradigm of sociability" extracted from his everyday experiences with "associations of the educated and the enlightened" in Edinburgh. This paradigm was to explain social bonds through the sympathetic sharing of passions and sentiments. This sharing becomes the "very currency of sociability."[5]

Hume attempts to show how this affective bond is elaborated not just in particular, small associations, but also in society at large. Sympathetic sharing works even for those who are "distant from us," as evidenced by the "uneasiness" we feel generally in cases of injustice. It is on the basis of such sympathy that we come to have "an extensive concern for society." Although humans may sometimes be motivated to behave justly on the basis of their self-interest, it is only this natural economy of the passions, Hume asserts, that gives our orientation to justice any long-term solidity.[6]

Although there is no direct evidence that Hume's ideas influenced Burke's thinking in the *Inquiry,* they help one get a sense of the general terrain on which Burke probably understood himself to be operating.[7] This is especially true of the question of exactly how the passions bind society together at different levels. An elucidation of the sketchy, even implicit answers Burke gives to this question in the *Inquiry* is crucial to understanding how he interprets the specific political issues he confronts later in his career.

In the *Inquiry* the primary focus is on the social bond between a man and a woman. What about bonds beyond this level? The answer in regard to circles of friends and other small groups—*"particular society"*—seems easy. Like Hume, Burke has no difficulty imagining the bonding force of pleasurable passions at this level: "Good company, lively conversations, and the endearments of friendship, fill the mind with great pleasure."[8] But at the level of "general *society,*" Burke seems a bit unsure. Mere social contact is likely sought more to avoid the fearfulness of complete solitude than for any real pleasure. And yet there seems to be some modicum of "social affection" even for those who are strangers. Again, like Hume, Burke refers us to our reactions to scenes of "distress," where that affection gives rise to "pity" and thus a motivation to relieve the suffering of others.[9]

There is at least one severe problem with this sort of account of the coherence of society. It is a problem with multiple implications, and one sees the outlines of some of Burke's most distinctive notions emerging out of his struggle with these implications. Mullan, speaking of Hume, expresses the overall difficulty succinctly when he suggests that the sort of approach shared by Hume and Burke obscures the potentially sharp "disparity between the immediate experience of sociability (conversation, the flow of affections, the communication of sentiments) and the implications of belonging to a political society."[10] For example, the bond of solidarity of a particular group may be strongly prejudicial to the well-being of the whole society. Politically this emerges as the problem of "factions" that so bothered thinkers in the eighteenth century.[11] Another difficulty is that the recourse to scenes of distress to prove the existence of extensive "social affection" at best gives that phenomenon a reality that may only be sporadically effective. Also, within society at large, what makes a situation one of distress? In the elucidation of his argument, Burke makes it seem that situations of distress strike us naturally like apples falling off trees. But he also implies elsewhere in the text that "second nature" may inure one person to all kinds of things that might be scenes of distress to another. Burke himself, throughout his life, cultivated an immunity to the "distress" of the poor, and yet he was thrown into a rage that others were not immediately and deeply affected by the fate of Marie Antoinette.[12]

Burke does have some resources in the *Inquiry* for meeting the deficits of social affection in large-scale society. One can infer that any lack is to be balanced by the sublimity of political authority. Governments dispose over instruments of power; and the threat of their use evokes the passions associated with the sublime, which in turn draws us back to our duties.[13] Burke cites the phrase traditionally used to address sovereigns, "dread majesty," to highlight the peculiar, intimate connection that exists in politics between fear, on the one hand, and awe and respect, on the other.[14]

When Burke entered political life, he soon found this sort of blanket answer to the problem of deficits of social affection to be unsatisfactory. His aesthetics was modified accordingly, as we shall see in a moment. Thus not only did Burke's aesthetics influence his political views, but the latter also induced changes in the former. It is to this two-way process that I now turn.

II. Entry Into Politics: 1765-1779

Although Burke was catapulted to the upper levels of British politics in 1765, with his entry into Parliament and Rockingham's brief tenure as leader of the government, he was never part of the real inner circle of power. That is hardly surprising, given his Irish background and modest circumstances. He was, however, a trusted adviser of the inner circle of Whig grandees, and along with William Dowdeswell, one of their most able speakers and strategists from the late 1760s to the early 1780s. His writings and speeches during this period are largely interpretations of the current political situation and recommendations about "what is to be done" from the Whig perspective. As one might expect, the basic stances he took were ones that had passed muster with the Whig leadership. But within this overall constraint, Burke crafted distinctive types of justifications for given policy positions. He wrote and spoke on almost every major topic of the day. I want to focus on three issues and examine the interplay between his political experience and his aesthetics. The issues are the nature of political parties, the relationship of Britain and its colonies, and the growing influence of the Crown.

In Burke's day there was of course nothing that resembled a contemporary political party. Whether outside or inside of Parliament, strong political coalitions ran the risk of being associated with the sinister motives of "faction." We have already seen how faction becomes a specific problem within Burke's own philosophical orientation. But it must also be remembered that the problem of faction had been one of the mainstay evils of the Western political imagination from classical Greece up to James Madison's famous "Number Ten" of the *Federalist Papers* in 1787.[15]

At this point in English parliamentary history, administrations were formed by the king, who picked individual, eminent members of Parliament with whom he felt comfortable to serve as ministers. When Rockingham was forced to resign as leader of the government in 1766, he and some of the other leading Whigs increasingly began to move toward the notion that none of them should individually join a new administration; rather they should wait until the king was ready to agree substantially to their terms in regard to both policy positions and personnel. Burke heartily endorsed this strategy.

In his first major piece of political writing, "Thoughts on the Present Discontents" (1770), Burke spoke of party as the organizational means to resolve certain festering political problems.[16] The most infamous of these concerned John Wilkes, whom the king and his supporters had denied a seat in Parliament in 1769, even though he had been duly elected by the constituents of Middlesex. This incident raised serious constitutional issues for many and occasioned substantial popular disturbance.

In Burke's mind there was no real need for constitutional reform. All of the present discontents could be alleviated if the members of the House of Commons and the public at large would support a return to power of Rockingham and his supporters. The organizational power of this group was proffered as the only effective barrier against the insidious growth of the system of "Influence," through which the Crown increased its power at the expense of the independence of Parliament and ultimately the freedom of the country.[17] The king and his behind-the-scenes advisers were, according to Burke, expanding the Crown's power by distributing lucrative jobs to those who would support them.

Later scholarship has shown that this threat was largely an imaginary one.[18] But the important point for the present context is that the Rockingham Whigs believed it was real and they constructed a self-image around that perception. They saw themselves as men of principle bound together for the public good. The power of party had become a necessity to break the power of "Influence."[19]

But Burke is recommending the political party not just in an instrumental sense. He considers it also to have an intrinsic value as an expression of human sociability in a free society. In effect, Burke redescribes the party on the analogy of friendship and other small social circles, suggesting that we "bring the dispositions that are lovely in private life into the service and conduct of the commonwealth." A party is bound together not just by common interests but also by "common affections."[20] Although Burke does not say so explicitly, the Rockingham party becomes in a real sense an object of beauty, standing in sharp contrast to the ugliness of its financially corrupt opponents.

It has sometimes been claimed that one of Burke's greatest contributions to political thought is the groundwork he lays for conceptualizing the modern political party.[21] This assertion is probably wrong for a couple of reasons. First, he was not the only one to be speaking more positively of parties. In reality, "Burke was rowing with the tide."[22] Second, his specific appeal to the "beauty" of party is fairly idiosyncratic, at least in terms of how parties have been thought of since then.

This appeal is more understandable when it is seen as an attempt to struggle with the problem of social affection and political society. Simply using the conceptual resources of the *Inquiry,* one would assume that Burke would look to the power of the sovereign to control the divisive force of faction. But the situation he saw in 1770 precluded that solution, for it was precisely the Crown's supporters who constituted the most dangerous faction. Burke's notion of a political party now can be seen as a new sort of solution. The binding passions of private "particular" societies, as analyzed in the *Inquiry,* are now projected onto an explicitly political grouping. These passions are worthy of public esteem and support; the hidden, greed-ridden ones of the court faction are, on the other hand, worthy only of condemnation.

As the tensions between Great Britain and its American colonies intensified in the 1770s, Burke was forced to reflect further on the issues of social affection and political society. How should one understand the bonds that underlie the relationship between colony and home country, and what can be done to cultivate them? Burke's answers in the case of America are quite different from those he gives in regard to India in the 1780s. (Within these differences, there are, however, certain common themes, as I will show in the next section.)

On one level Burke sees the growing tension with America as an eminently avoidable result of bad British policies and of the intellectual recourse on both sides to abstract, "metaphysical" thinking. Political prudence was giving way to intransigence, attached on the American side to claims of natural rights being denied by the colonizer, and on the British side to dogged assertions of the sovereign right of the British government to rule its colonies as it saw fit. Burke, as he always did, criticized this infusion of metaphysical thinking into politics. But in this controversy, he did not yet see such infusion as part of the problematic of a new epoch, the way he did in the 1780s. What guides Burke's analysis of the outbreak of war is his perception of an degenerative dialectic of social affection and government action. Although Burke does not explicitly use the language of tyranny, his writings in general during the 1770s sketch a portrait of the Crown and its supporters as tending in that direction. In effect, what Burke is being forced to do is to separate more carefully than in the *Inquiry* what distinguishes legitimate from illegitimate political authority. There he had simply associated authority with the sublime and summed up this insight with his reference to "dread majesty." But in "Thoughts" he admits the possibility that political authority may be "at once dreaded *and* condemned."[23]

Thus, Burke wants the fear that is inspired by tyrannical politics to be sharply distinguished from the authentic sublimity of legitimate politics. A tyrant is indeed fearful up close, but "distance" does not transform that in any salutary manner, as is supposed to be the case with an object of the sublime. Distance in this case only allows space for condemnation and "abhorrence."[24] Moreover, one may be humbled by a tyrant, but the effect of *this* humility is hardly wisdom.

In the years leading up to the American Revolution, the British government looked increasingly to a policy of intimidation in order to bring the colonies back into submission. In his "Speech on Conciliation With America" in 1775, Burke charges that such a course of action only undermines the social bond that is the real foundation of Great Britain's "hold" over its colonies: "Close affection . . . grows from common names, from kindred blood, from similar privileges, and equal protection. These are ties which, though light as air, are as strong as links of iron."[25] But governments can corrode these links by abusive policies. Against the recourse to "absolute power," he suggests that authority is "sometimes bought by kindness" and "magnanimity."[26]

Two important insights are emerging here. First, extensive society is now seen as holding together over the long run rather like the smaller, particular society Burke spoke of in the *Inquiry*. Perhaps he still believes in some universal residuum of fellow feeling, such as is displayed in scenes of distance distress; but that is not what effectively binds political societies. The real "cement" is the sharing of *particularities* that "second nature" makes possible and that in turn continually reproduce that nature. This sharing of particular memories, institutions, privileges, interests, and opinions—in short, "the spirit of English communion"—is the soil in which "close affection" thrives. This insight gives rise to another. Social affection at this degree of extension will have to be mediated by imaginative representation far more than at lesser degrees, where common particularities are shared face to face. This means that extensive affection is far more susceptible to dissolution and thus far more in need of conscious cultivation by political institutions.[27]

One might phrase these points in the metaphor of theater. In the *Reformer,* where Burke donned the hat of theater critic, he had shown himself to be very concerned with the influence of theater on public sentiments and morals. In his political career, he often thought of the activity of governing as an ongoing performance. The view of aesthetic-affective dynamics emerging from the *Inquiry* would have assigned to government a fairly simple and mechanical role: overawing the populace. What Burke recognized in the 1770s, however, is that government has a more complex role to play if it is to foster imaginatively the bond of social affection in the populace. Thus when he assails the actions of the government towards America in this period, he is in effect once again a theater critic, only this time he is berating the star actor for misconstruing its role—although the critic himself was not clear on the nature of the role until the play actually commenced.

Burke's new thinking about the role of government is again highlighted in his "Letter to the Sheriffs of Bristol" in 1777. With war now a reality, Burke surveys the actions that led up to it. But he is speaking, at least implicitly, not just to the American issue, but to the whole course of government decisions within England as well, from the Wilkes affair to the suspension of habeas corpus after the outbreak of war. The primary fault of the government is now strikingly identified as its unwillingness to display virtues that the *Inquiry* had called feminine and "domestic": "the amiable and conciliatory virtues of lenity, moderation, and tenderness."[28]

Thus, over the course of the 1760s and 1770s, Burke interpreted new political experiences to a substantial degree in terms of his understanding of aesthetic-affective dynamics. But he also introduced important modifications of his aesthetics as it applies to social life. The relatively neat, isomorphic mapping of the beautiful and sublime onto the private and public, as well as female and male, has been heavily revised. The public, political value of beautiful/private/female characteristics has been recognized as crucial for maintaining the strength of social affection across large populations. This process of revaluation in Burke's thought proceeds, however, without any rethinking of the relationship of women to public life.

As Burke elevates the passions of the beautiful into the public sphere, he simultaneously creates increasing pressure on his understanding of the sublime. His condemnation of the British government forces him in the direction of having to become more explicit about the moral-political criteria for judging what is a perversion of the sublime in public life, and what is an authentic embodiment. He now resists the implication emerging from the *Inquiry* that power, terror, and intimidation per se are adequate to evoke the sort of subjective experience he associates with the sublime.

III. The 1780s and the Emergence of Political Modernity

As Burke began to comprehend the outlines of political modernity, these processes of rethinking continued. The issue of British rule in India, at least as it is crystallized in the Hastings trial, would appear to be largely remote from the sorts of dangers that Burke was to find in the French Revolution. And yet, as noted in Chapter 1, Burke saw Hastings as the archetype of a character who was forcing his way onto the political stage in the modern world: the individual whose appetite and will face neither internal nor external limits. The threat Burke referred to as "Indianism" was that this character and his ethos, nurtured in a distant land, would begin to infect public life in England.

Although Burke saw Hastings as a novel, dangerous type who threatened the future, for the impeachment proceedings Hastings and his advisers chose to describe his actions in a way that allowed him recognition as a venerable character within the tradition of Western political thought. Hastings, they argued, was acting as a despot where despotism was appropriate: in the Orient. Ever since the ancient Greeks had created the contrast between themselves as free by nature and the Persians as slavelike by nature, Europeans had perpetuated the belief that despotism was the mode of authority proper for Asian peoples. Hastings, as a colonial governor, was merely giving the peoples of India what was fitting. And that meant a government that need not show any virtues except effectiveness, understood simply as maintaining obedience through fear.

Burke responds by attempting to demolish the traditional, Western image of the Eastern "Other." To do this, he steeped himself in knowledge of India. His claim is that the despotism model is merely a convenient fraud, rooted in a willful refusal to look carefully at the complex traditions and institutions of India.[29] Although Burke showed great respect throughout his life for Montesquieu, here he flatly rejects the great French political theorist's support for such a notion of political authority.[30]

This bold rejection of Oriental despotism is a significant step in Western political thought. But at the very moment that Burke dissolves this traditional "Other" of the West, he constructs another, more subtle one to take its place. India, as Burke portrays it in the trial before the House of Lords, is a land of beauty, inhabited by gentle and somewhat helpless peoples. She is, in short, a woman, to whom the colonizers owe care and protection.[31] Burke's gendered refiguration of the proper relationship with India allows him to deploy a new, incisive argument against Hastings. The notion of despotism is now unmasked as a simple disguise for brutal sexual assault. Hastings and his cohorts were involved in nothing less than the rape of India.[32] The question Burke wishes to frame for Hastings's judges reduces to: Are the British rapists of other lands or gentlemen protectors?

Of course, even if the Lords had chosen the latter image, they would still have been keeping India within a clear model of subordination. But the subordination would have been, as it were, "all in the family"; an imagined bond of social affection would have made the phenomenon of domination less glaring, at least to the colonizers. Master and servant would be joined within a domesticated aesthetic of the sublime and the beautiful, male and female.

However unappealing this model of authority sounds to contemporary ears, it is important to emphasize that Burke thought it was an improvement on the one Hastings proposed. Burke's hostility to despotism here parallels his hostility to the creeping tyranny of the Crown. Both instances forced him away from any simple identification of the sublime with the exercise of limitless power in politics. This turn in his thinking is crucial to notice, if we are to make sense of his later understanding of politics and aesthetics. More than one discussion of Burke's notion of the sublime has missed this turn, identifying the Burkean sublime simply with something like "lawless masculine force."[33]

The fact that such an identification is incorrect is also evident when one considers Burke's thoughts on execution. In Chapter 1, I suggested that the Gordon Riots of 1780 had a profound influence on Burke. After restoring order at that time, the government set about the task of apprehending and punishing the instigators. Keeping in mind the degree to which Burke was shaken by this display of popular fury, one could easily imagine him relishing the opportunity for "dread majesty" to inscribe its "lawless masculine force" on the rioters in a terrifying spectacle of counterfury. But Burke reacted negatively to the planned executions of large numbers of individuals. Moreover, his reflections here have none of that macabre enthusiasm one finds in a conservative like Joseph deMaistre, for example, when it comes to executing disturbers of law and order.[34]

Burke tried to persuade Lord North's government to think carefully about the punishment meted out to the rioters. He feared that the government's anger and concern to appear powerful would result in a multitude of executions. Just as in the case of the American colonies, so also here Burke thought that a show of overwhelming power was unwise: "I have ever observed that the execution of one man fixes the attention and excites awe, the execution of multitudes dissipates and weakens the effect."[35] The latter policy cannot help appearing excessive and arbitrary, and the effect of that will only be to "irritate" those who are positively disposed toward the "general spirit of the tumults."[36]

What is ultimately at stake for Burke in this situation is the continued capacity of the British political system to excite awe, to induce an experience of the true sublime in its population; and what hangs on that is its ability to defeat the "spirit" of popular tumult that animated the riots. As I pointed out earlier, after the outbreak of the French Revolution Burke looked back at this "spirit" of 1780 and identified it as the germ of English Jacobinism. Whether Burke saw things in exactly this epochal light only a few weeks after the Gordon Riots is debatable. But even if he did not, it is significant that he already envisioned a deep interrelationship between the sustenance of an authentic experience of the sublime in political life and the danger of unleashed collective will.

By the time of his "Speech on the State of Representation," in May 1782, it is clear that Burke had come to a striking realization that there was an epochal quality to the eruptions of popular will he was witnessing.[37] Before turning to this speech, I want to illustrate more precisely the sense in which Burke understood the changes around him as "epochal." As I have shown, in his reflections on the American problem Burke ultimately pointed the finger of blame at the British government. His assignment of responsibility there was grounded in a general interpretation of the causes of "disorders of the people." The American rebellion, he asserted in his

1777 "Address to the King," resulted from "the *usual and natural cause* of such disorders at all times and in all places, where such have prevailed—the misconduct of government." It is only such official behavior that can "convert into fear and hatred that habitual reverence ever paid by mankind to an ancient and venerable government."[38] Thus, for Burke, disorders of the people are an easily understandable, dependent variable in the "natural" dynamics of political life.

What he comes to comprehend with a jolt in 1782, is that such disorders are taking on a more independent, intransigent life. In effect, the natural, causal connections of "normal" politics are giving way. Something radically new is emerging in history. His awareness of this novelty and its dangerousness emerge in both the tone and substance of his speech on the reform of parliamentary representation.

Burke had never been a friend of the idea of electoral reform. His initial position was one of skepticism and mild opposition. Proponents of reform were not, he contended, adequately considering things like the possible unintended outcomes of their schemes. This stance changed sharply, however, when in the spring of 1782, a new round of reform proposals was brought before Parliament. The danger, Burke implied, was now no longer fuzzy-headed reform but a lurking monster. He startled his audience with the vehemence of his attack. Even a parliamentary ally, Richard Sheridan, accused him on this occasion of the "most magnanimous indiscretion." He said that Burke attacked his opponents in a "scream of passion."[39] Part of the explanation of Burke's new hostility to the reformers might lay in the fact that Rockingham had in early 1782 just taken over as leader of a new, Whig administration, in which Burke held the relatively lucrative office of paymaster general of the forces. Burke, who no doubt thought of this new government as the champion of administrative reform, would hardly have welcomed the reemergence of the political reform proposals at this moment. He likely smelled an attempt by Rockingham's opponents to embarrass the new prime minister.

However, even if one tries to explain away the vehemence of Burke's speech as a reflection of the pressures of immediate political infighting, that cannot explain the distinctive *content* of the speech. That quickly brings us back to the suspicion that Burke sensed something of great magnitude. As one Burke scholar notes—but does little to clarify—almost all of the fundamental ideas that Burke was to employ later in his criticism of the French Revolution are already present in this speech in 1782.[40]

Burke's speech largely ignores the specific proposals for reform; rather, attention is riveted on what he is now convinced is the *necessary* tendency toward anarchy of all proposals for changing the constitution. They all have such a necessity, because they are all nourished by the spread of a malignant "humor." Those affected by this humor see the political world as a domain for the unlimited acceleration of reason and will. Burke is startled to realize that suddenly the British constitution, which for much of the eighteenth century had been the object of "the admiration and envy of the world," is now being transformed before his eyes into a "gross imposition upon the understanding of mankind, an insult to their feelings." What permits this transformation is the loss of a sense of "reverence" for traditional institutions that is corroded away by the speculations of the new "political architects."[41] Once this corrosion begins to work, the constitution will collapse under the weight of the first substantial popular disorders.

Near the conclusion of the speech, Burke announces what in effect becomes the motto of his life from that point on: "It is to this humor . . . that I set myself . . . in the most determined opposition."[42] What is especially interesting here is that Burke's own earlier analysis of aesthetic-affective dynamics has shown how difficult this task of holding together the traditional order is going to be.

Burke was always aware of the powerful affect that custom and tradition have. One of the most often quoted lines from the *Inquiry* is: "Custom reconciles us to everything."[43] It is in this sense that he refers to custom as "second nature." But Burke was also aware in the *Inquiry* that this glue had its weaknesses. Custom may determine our behavior, but we are also likely to feel toward what is customary "a stale *unaffecting* familiarity" or "indifference."[44] In saying this Burke is, curiously enough, implying that the more undisturbed a society's traditions remain over time the more susceptible people become to being attracted to novel ideas and schemes. Along these same lines he suggests that "it is the nature of things that hold us by custom, to affect us very little whilst we are in possession of them, but strongly when they are absent."[45] Burke makes these remarks in the context of a technical argument about the notion of beauty. One might be tempted to claim therefore that they really have nothing directly to do with reflections on the constitution of political society. Many years later, however, in his 1791 "Appeal From the New to the Old Whigs," he makes precisely the same argument about not appreciating traditional institutions until they are endangered.[46] This makes it quite plausible to conceive of Burke in 1782 as coming to realize that his own analysis in the *Inquiry* points to the conclusion that venerable political institutions alone are not adequate anchors for order and authority, even when the government refrains from active misconduct. When this insight is combined with his growing awareness of the necessity of separating a politics that evokes an authentic sublime from one that evokes merely fear and dread, one gets a sense of the dimensions of the problem Burke was facing in 1782, when he tries to articulate a strategy for combating political modernity.

One can also now fully appreciate the extraordinary significance of the metaphor he employs in the concluding lines of his speech on reform. There he declares that:

> I look with filial reverence on the Constitution of my country, and never will cut it in pieces, and put it into the kettle of any magician, in order to boil it, with the puddle of their compounds, into youth and vigor. On the contrary, I will drive away such pretenders; I will nurse its venerable age, and with lenient arts extend a parent's breath.[47]

When Burke reflected upon the bond of social affection in the 1770s, he focused his attention on things the government should and should not do. From this point in the early 1780s, until the end of his life, he was even more concerned with the public's own understanding of its relationship to the basic constitutive institutions of society and polity. In other words, not only did the government have to cultivate certain feminine, domestic virtues, but the people had to cultivate an attachment to their traditions that would counterbalance the natural tendency to indifference and the resultant susceptibility to novelty—especially when it comes in the form of "metaphysical" doctrines such as natural rights that carry within them such a powerful momentum away from encumbrance and particularity.

The preceding quotation reveals the image around which Burke thought such attachment could be fostered. The image is a familial one: Political traditions become the aged parent and the people become the child physician called upon to attend to that parent's infirmities.[48] Two things about this metaphor are crucial.

First, the metaphor is the same one that appears later in *Reflections on the Revolution in France.*[49] Burke, by 1782, thus appears to have set into place some reconceptualizations that remain with him from that point on. Part of this involves a strong appeal to our imagination. As he puts it explicitly in the *Reflections,* we must imaginatively bind up "the constitution of our country with our dearest domestic ties." Political health in the modern world cannot be rooted in unthinking traditionalism, but rather only in affirmative "choice" to attach ourselves to our collective inheritance.[50]

The inevitable *fact* that we are "encumbered" selves is thus only a starting point; learning to affirm that encumbrance requires the imaginative reweaving of aesthetic-affective dynamics.[51] What exactly, though, is the pattern to look like? Here it is instructive to contrast the way Burke envisions the family in 1782, with the way he envisioned it in the passage from the *Inquiry* quoted in the preceding chapter (p. 33). There the mother is the object of beauty attracting affection from the child and the father is the object of sublimity evoking respect and fear. The grandfather is held up as an aesthetic-affective hybrid. His power, unlike the father's, is attenuated. His age places him in need of help and protection; in effect, he exhibits a "weakness and imperfection" that feminizes him.[52]

When these aesthetic-affective relationships within the family are drawn upon for reconceptualizing public relationships in 1782, they undergo some significant shifts. And it is in these shifts that one sees Burke's image of an authentic sublime emerging. As I have already shown, from the time he entered public life, he began to back away from the simple, stark identification of the sublime with what is merely overpowering: what is above and immensely threatening. Now Burke clearly indicates that authentic sublimity is less intimately associated with a spatial relation (over/under) and more intimately associated with a temporal one (past/present). In 1782, it is no longer the father towering over the child who is the archetype of the sublime, with the grandfather as merely a diluted form. Now it is the aged parent who is the archetype. As with the earlier image of the grandfather, age is what is crucial, not power. But it is important to note also that the new archetype is not gendered. In this change, another crucial shift is signaled.

The grandfather of the *Inquiry* lightly evokes the sublime, because he palely reflects the father's power. His feminine "weakness and imperfection" also allow the child simultaneously to feel strong affection. In the modified image of the aged parent and child, however, sublimity is evoked not from the attenuated power of the former, but rather from how its age evokes reflections about the latter's own limited power and finitude. The child is cast as a physician who understands that what is aged must be *cared for;* there is ultimately no *cure.* Agedness is now no longer an "imperfection" that simply dilutes sublimity, a weakness the male child sees as foreign to his nature. Rather the agedness of the parent evokes humility, for it highlights our ungendered, common humanity: our mortality. The parent closer to death vivifies our own finitude. This remains for Burke the core of the authentically sublime. In sum then, the full image of the aged parent and child physician has the effect of repositioning death—the *Inquiry*'s "king of terrors"—in Burke's aesthetic-affective dynamics so that its presence is now to be felt more quietly but more pervasively.

At this point in his life, Burke is still in one sense very close to his ideas in the *Inquiry*, but in another sense very distant from them. He is still close— and will always remain so—in that his confrontation with political life continues to be interpreted through his aesthetic-affective categories. He is distant, however, in that those categories have undergone important shifts. His clear binaries—sublime/beautiful, public/private, and male/female— have become blurred, as he has attempted to develop a more sophisticated understanding of politics. Moreover, in the 1780s, these shifts can increasingly be seen as responses to Burke's growing perception of the epochal challenge of political modernity. Thus when the French Revolution breaks out in 1789, Burke is in a fundamental conceptual sense ready for it. He understands what kind of underlying affective orientation a people must have toward its traditional institutions. And he understands that the strength of such an orientation will depend increasingly on conscious cultivation and choice.

Notes

1. Christopher Reid, *Edmund Burke and the Practice of Political Writing* (New York: St. Martin's, 1985), p. 38.

2. See, for example, W. J. T. Mitchell, "Eye and Ear: Edmund Burke and the Politics of Sensibility," in *Iconology: Image, Text, Ideology* (Chicago: University of Chicago Press, 1986), pp. 129-145. In looking directly from the *Inquiry* to the *Reflections,* Mitchell thinks Burke's views on the sublime can be shown to be inconsistent. This problem is dissolved when one attends closely to the writings that come between these two; pp. 132ff.

3. For a discussion of these different views of passion, see John Mullan, *Sentiment and Sociability: The Language of Feeling in the Eighteenth Century* (Oxford, U.K.: Clarendon Press, 1988), Introduction and Chap. 1.

4. David Hume, *A Treatise of Human Nature,* ed. L. A. Selby-Bigge & P. H. Nidditch (Oxford, U.K.: Clarendon Press, 1978).

5. Mullan, *Sentiment and Sociability,* pp. 3, 24.

6. Hume, *A Treatise,* pp. 498-99, 579; and Mullan, *Sentiment and Sociability,* p. 34.

7. It is generally accepted that the introductory essay "On Taste," which Burke added to the second edition of the *Inquiry,* was influenced by Hume's own essay on that subject. See, for example, J. T. Boulton, "Editor's Introduction" in Edmund Burke's *A Philosophical Enquiry Into the Origin of Our Ideas of the Sublime and Beautiful,* ed. with introduction and notes by J. T. Boulton (New York: Columbia University Press, 1958), pp. xxviii-xxix. As to whether Burke had actually read Hume's *A Treatise of Human Nature* when he originally composed the *Inquiry,* however, there is no clear evidence. Cf. Herbert Wickelns, "Burke's Essay 'On the Sublime and the Beautiful': An Annotated Edition" (Unpublished doctoral dissertation, Cornell University, 1922), pp. lxvii, 339-42.

8. *Inquiry, Works,* I, p. 116.

9. Ibid., pp. 115, 118-19.

10. Mullan, *Sentiment and Sociability,* p. 34.

11. See, for example, Mullan's discussion of the third Earl of Shaftesbury; *Sentiment and Sociability,* pp. 26-27.

12. See Burke's discussion of the poor in "A Vindication of Natural Society" (1756), *Works,* I, pp. 58ff; and "Thoughts and Details on Scarcity" (1795), *Works,* V, pp. 134ff.

13. *Inquiry, Works,* I, p. 113.

14. Ibid., p. 141. Burke refers to the way the ancient Greeks retained this dual connotation; p. 131. Perhaps he remembers Plutarch's comments to the effect that political authority in Sparta was rooted in a potent mixture of fear and respect. See Plutarch, *Plutarch on Sparta,* trans. with introduction by Richard J. A. Talbert (London: Penguin, 1988), pp. 77-78.

15. *The Federalist Papers,* ed. Clinton Rossiter (New York: New American Library, 1961) pp. 77-84.

16. "Thoughts on the Present Discontents" (1770), *WS,* II, pp. 314ff.

17. Ibid., pp. 258-60.

18. Paul Langford, "Introduction," *WS,* II, p. 17.

19. "Thoughts," *WS,* II, pp. 314-15.

20. Ibid., pp. 317, 320.

21. Carl B. Cone, *Burke and the Nature of Politics: The Age of the American Revolution* (Lexington: University of Kentucky Press, 1957).

22. Langford, "Introduction," p. 12.

23. "Thoughts," *WS,* II, p. 253. My emphasis.

24. Ibid.

25. "Speech on Conciliation With America" (1775), *Works,* II, p. 179.

26. Ibid., p. 181.

27. Ibid., pp. 179-80; Cf. *Corr.,* III, p. 432.

28. "Letter to the Sheriffs of Bristol" (1777), *Works,* II, pp. 235, 244.

29. Although Burke tried to paint a picture of India as a place where traditions and institutions were in good order, that does not appear to have been the case; see C. P. Courtney, *Montesquieu and Burke* (Westport, CT: Greenwood, 1975 reprint), p. 131. If this was so, *and* one was committed, like Burke, to maintaining British rule, then his blanket condemnation of

Hastings's use of force and manipulation loses some of its power. Cf. P. J. Marshall, *The Impeachment of Warren Hastings* (Oxford: Oxford University Press, 1965), pp. 180-91.

30. "Speech in General Reply, May 28, 1794," *Works,* XI, pp. 194-96, 203-7; Cf. Courtney, *Montesquieu and Burke,* pp. 139-40.

31. "Speech on Opening of Impeachment, February 1788," *WS,* VI, pp. 301-4; 345-47.

32. For a good discussion of the sexual imagery in Burke's attack on Hastings, see Isaac Kramnick, *The Rage of Edmund Burke: Portrait of an Ambivalent Conservative* (New York: Basic Books, 1977), Chap. 7.

33. Terry Eagleton, *The Ideology of the Aesthetic* (Oxford, U.K.: Basil Blackwell, 1990), p. 54. Cf. Kramnick's overidentification of the sublime with ambition, especially that of the bourgeois men of talents in the eighteenth century; *The Rage of Edmund Burke,* pp. 94-95.

34. Consider deMaistre's remark that "all grandeur, all power, all subordination rests on the executioner: he is the horror and the bond of human association"; "The Saint Petersburg Dialogues," in *The Works of Joseph deMaistre,* trans. and introduced by J. Lively (London: Allen & Unwin, 1965), p. 192. It is useful to draw a contrast between Burke and deMaistre, because it allows one to resist the idea that Burke's views on politics, punishment, and the sublime can be easily subsumed under Foucault's notion of monarchical power, illustrated so memorably by the description of Damiens' execution at the beginning of *Discipline and Punish* (New York: Random House, 1979). DeMaistre's views would indeed fit this model of the bloody inscription of the monarch's will on the body of the offender. Burke's, I think, would not. His variant of "official theater" has a peculiarly eighteenth-century English quality to it, in the sense of an awareness of the significance of limits. Even though the acts that called forth public executions were by definition ones that went beyond normal social limits, Burke's thinking on this subject shows a concern for the regime's responding with a carefully measured and moderate show of power. Cf. E. P. Thompson, "Patrician Society, Plebian Culture," *Journal of Social History,* Summer 1984, pp. 382-405.

Burke actually makes a brief reference to the execution of Damiens in the second edition of the *Inquiry,* to suggest that aversion to pain is a stronger force than attraction to pleasure; *Works,* II, pp. 110-11.

35. "Some Thoughts on the Approaching Executions" (1780), *Works,* VI, p. 247. These thoughts were conveyed to the Lord Chancellor in the month following the riots.

36. Ibid., p. 246; and "Some Additional Reflections on the Executions" (1780), *Works,* VI, p. 252.

37. "Speech on the State of Representation" (1782), *Works,* VII, pp. 89-104.

38. "Address to the King" (1777), *Works,* VI, p. 163. My emphasis.

39. Quoted in Stanley Ayling, *Edmund Burke: His Life and Opinions* (New York: St. Martin's, 1988), p. 116.

40. C. P. Courtney, *Montesquieu and Burke,* p. 142.

41. "Speech on the State of Representation," p. 91.

42. Ibid., p. 103.

43. *Inquiry, Works,* II, p. 231. This line stands alone on the cover of a recent edition of the *Inquiry,* as if it somehow sums up the essence of that work; see Adam Phillips, ed., *A Philosophical Enquiry* (Oxford: Oxford University Press, 1990).

44. Ibid., pp. 102, 180. My emphasis.

45. Ibid., pp. 179-80.

46. "Appeal from the New to the Old Whigs," *Works,* IV, p. 76.

47. "Speech on the State of Representation," *Works,* VII, p. 104. Burke had used this metaphor on one previous occasion; see "Speech on Economical Reform" (1780), *Works,* II, p. 302.

48. The role of child physician would for Burke be restricted, of course, only to those already politically enfranchised.

49. "Reflections on the Revolution in France," *WS,* VIII, p. 146.

50. Ibid., p. 84. Cf. David Bromwich, *A Choice of Inheritance: Self and Community From Edmund Burke to Robert Frost* (Cambridge, MA: Harvard University Press, 1989), pp. 45-59.

51. I borrow the notion of "encumbered" selves from Michael Sandel, *Liberalism and the Limits of Justice* (Cambridge: Cambridge University Press, 1982).

52. *Inquiry, Works,* II, pp. 115-16, 188, 190.

4

Confronting the French Revolution

W hen Burke composed *Reflections on the Revolution in France,* his primary intention was to warn his own country about the immense danger looming across the channel. Every rhetorical skill that he had honed during three decades on the political stage was brought to bear on his new task. In this work and those that followed it, Burke tried to demonstrate in every way possible why the revolution constituted a deadly assault on the basic values of English political life. This demonstration is repeated through skillful deployments of a succession of traditional idioms by which the English had interpreted their political world. The revolution is indicted for among other things, creating a paper money despotism, endangering the "ancient constitution" with its heritage of English freedom, and reviving that uncontrollable spiritual "enthusiasm" that had been responsible for the horrors of the English Civil War a century before.[1]

This image of Burke as a master of the grammars of traditional English political discourse is essential to any full appreciation of his thinking on revolution. But the question I wish to raise is whether this image by itself does not ease Burke a little too securely into the ranks of minor figures in the history of political thought. Perhaps Burke's genius is a bit more distinctive. What is needed is a perspective that can somehow bring this out without at the same time entangling one in the opposite sort of error: according Burke the mantle of a prophet who divined the threat of totalitarianism with inexplicable prescience. Conor Cruise O'Brien goes so far in this regard as to speak of *"perception extrasensorielle."*[2] It is indeed true that when Burke warned his readers of the danger arising in France, the actual onset of the Terror was still over two years away. Long before the guillotine began to cut and denunciation became the daily bread of Parisian public life, Burke felt the beginnings of the momentum toward that end. Nevertheless, recourse to terms like "clairvoyance" and "prophesy" may have a tendency to deaden interpretation. A prophet "sees" with the aid of something mysterious or divine; a political thinker "sees" with the aid of a context. The alternative I have been pursuing so far in this book is to sketch a distinctive intellectual context, or language game, within which Burke had been operating before the French Revolution. It was certainly not a "private" language game; but it also was not one in which the political public generally participated. It is against this background of his reflections on aesthetics and political modernity that one can comprehend Burke's perceptions of the revolution in a fashion that on the one hand recognizes their brilliance without on the other hand making them unduly mysterious.

This perspective yields some novel insights not only about *what* Burke thinks is the nature of the epochal danger, but also about *how* he comes to perceive it. At issue is the process by which he comes to understand the events in France as the full historical embodiment of the threat whose specter he had already seen in England in the early 1780s (Section I). I explain why, for Burke, at the heart of the French Revolution there is an active perversion of aesthetic life, the most disturbing feature of which is the emergence of a false sublime (Section II). Finally, I turn briefly to Burke's notion of what constitutes an authentic sublime: one that would make us less susceptible to the dangers of political modernity (Section III).

I. Overwhelming Momentum

Jacobinism represented for Burke an attack on almost every institution he esteemed: established religion, traditional constitutional arrangements, and secure property, especially the entailed property that helped preserve

the landed elite who were the best sources of political wisdom in a country.[3] If we focus too much on Burke's defense of these specific targets of
revolutionary action, however, we run the risk of not grasping clearly
enough what Burke feels is the common, animating spirit behind all such
assaults. In this regard, a letter from 1795 is perhaps the most informative
of all his many attempts to distill the essence of Jacobinism: "What is
Jacobinism? It is an attempt . . . to eradicate prejudice out of the minds of
men."[4]

Prejudice is the attachment one feels for established practices and institutions. It provides these things with a reservoir of resistance to the imperative immediacy of rational critique. Burke's aim is not to laud every
prejudice an individual or society expresses; indeed, he has no difficulty
speaking disparagingly of "vulgar," "false," and "antiquated prejudices."
His intention rather is to defend the "latent wisdom" of those prejudices
that seem to him crucial for holding together an ordered society.[5] It is the
total denial of the very possibility of any such wisdom by the Jacobins that
so enrages Burke, for it means that the pursuit of virtue in politics will
carry with it no sense of humility, and thus nothing that can dampen its
arrogance. "True humility," he writes, "is the low, but deep and firm foundation of all real virtue. But this, as very painful in the practice, and little
imposing in appearance, [the Jacobins] have totally discarded."[6]

When Burke first speaks at length about the significance of prejudice (in
the *Reflections*), his primary references leave no doubt that we are squarely
on the terrain of his aesthetics. Referring to the prejudices of the English,
he asserts that "We fear God; we look up with awe to kings, with affection
to parliaments, with duty to magistrates, with reverence to priests, and
with respect to nobility."[7] This precise mapping of passions and sentiments
onto corresponding objects is probably to a large degree an artifact of style;
Burke does not use such a map anywhere else. What is far more important
here is that we see the fundamental connection Burke wants to establish
between Jacobinism, prejudice, and the feelings associated with the sublime.

How did Burke come to this understanding of what lay behind the tur-
moil in France? The first expression of his feelings on the revolution came
in a letter to an Irish acquaintance on August 9, 1789:

> As to us here our thoughts of every thing at home are suspended, by our
> astonishment at the wonderful Spectacle which is exhibited in a Neighbour-
> ing and rival Country—what Spectators, and what actors! England gazing

with astonishment at a French struggle for Liberty and not knowing whether to blame or to applaud! The thing indeed, though I thought *I saw something like it in progress for several years,* has still something in it paradoxical and Mysterious. The spirit it is impossible not to admire; but the old Parisian *ferocity* has broken out in a shocking manner. It is true, that this may be no more than a sudden explosion: If so no indication can be taken from it. But if it should be character rather than accident, then that people are not fit for Liberty, and must have a Strong hand like that of their former masters to coerce them. Men must have *a certain fund of natural moderation* to qualify them for Freedom, else it become noxious to themselves and a perfect Nuisance to every body else. What will be the Event it is hard I think still to say.[8]

Clearly Burke, like many others throughout Europe, was astonished by the outbreak of revolution in France. But Burke's own astonishment and indecision about whether to "blame or applaud" should not be taken as an indication that he was at a loss for a context in which to consider what was unfolding before him. The danger is one that he knows: "I saw something like it in progress for several years." The "it" in this case is, I would argue, precisely that novel mix of abstract political ideas and popular will that so startled Burke in the early 1780s in England.[9] At that time he had seen the specter of something more than the traditional, episodic eruption of popular or crowd violence. He now ponders whether the violence in Paris during summer 1789 might be the result of "character not accident." What possesses "ferocity" by character can easily build momentum.

But in August, Burke is not yet certain that he is confronted with a people, who as he later puts it, are "from system furious."[10] When he wrote the letter quoted above, he had already seen substantial revolutionary changes in the political institutions of France. In June, what had been the separate Estates of the realm—nobility and Church, on the one hand, and commoners, on the other—were merged for purposes of representation in the new National Assembly. And on August 4, the feudal system of special rights for the nobility was abolished. Even if Burke had not heard of the latter event when he wrote his letter of August 9, the former alone was certainly comparable in magnitude to the electoral reform proposals he had so feared earlier in England. And yet Burke does not at this point pronounce a definitive negative judgment. He is apparently still willing to believe that there may yet be that "fund of natural moderation" in the French that is essential to the maintenance of liberty.[11] Burke is here making a general reference to natural, aesthetic-affective dynamics, more particularly the role of the sublime in restraining popular attacks on the state and social hierarchy. Perhaps, he reasons, this "fund" is still sufficient to counteract the momentum of political modernity.

This hope was soon shattered. On October 5 and 6, a large crowd marched from Paris to the palace at Versailles, seized Louis XVI and Marie Antoinette, and forced them to return to the city where they could be more easily kept under control. This event, and Burke's portrayal of the plight of Marie Antoinette, figures so centrally in the *Reflections* that it seems quite plausible to see it as the phenomenon that turned Burke into an implacable opponent of revolution. But the Versailles seizure was preceded by another occurrence, and there are good reasons to believe that it may have played the decisive role.

In 1773 Burke had visited France, at least partially for the purpose of depositing his son Richard with the Parisots, a prominent family at Auxerre in Burgundy, where he was to stay for several months to learn French. The elder Burke enjoyed his stay in Auxerre (far more than his visit with the elite of Paris on the same trip), and the two families developed a close friendship that was maintained through correspondence over the succeeding years. On September 14, 1789, Madame Parisot sent Richard a letter describing her plight during the "Great Fear" that was spreading through various parts of the French countryside in the late summer of that year. This was a period of intense anxiety and often mass hysteria characterized by food riots, roving bands of brigands, rumors of foreign invasion, and peasants pillaging estates. Madame Parisot gave the Burkes a vivid account of her family's experience at this time:

> The murderers and incendiaries have not yet reached us. However, we were warned that there were five or six hundred of them near us so we were obliged to flee, leaving our harvests and our house to the risk of pillage. [My daughter] took refuge in the vineyards, crouched on the damp ground in the rain for two hours, while we had to consider which way we would flee, prepare the horses and our servants, and leave. We went towards Auxerre and met only troops of frightened, armed inhabitants on the way. The warnings did not prove true for us. Upon other cantons, however, rage was indeed visited.[12]

Shortly after his son passed this letter on to him, Burke wrote a letter to a young friend and fellow member of Parliament, William Windham, who had just returned from Paris. Windham had given him an optimistic view of events there. Burke's letter brushes Windham's evidence aside and asserts that the revolution can do nothing but gather violent momentum; anyone in France who stands in the way will sooner or later be hung from a lamppost.[13] Given the fact that this letter is often pointed to as the place where Burke sets his face firmly against the revolution, one naturally wonders what exactly occasions the shift.[14] Curiously enough, if one examines the letter seeking the evidence Burke employs to dampen his young colleague's optimism, the only specific piece one finds is a reference to the Parisot letter. Burke tells his friend that it "paints the miserable and precarious situation of all people of property in dreadful colours."[15] The Parisot letter apparently was not, for Burke, just one more piece of political news, but rather an aesthetic-affective jolt, on the basis of which he felt he could thenceforth speak definitively about France. Why did this letter have such significance?

In the *Inquiry*, Burke had discussed how scenes of distress evoke a natural response of pity; and they are all the more affecting the more the sufferer is someone who has fallen from an elevated social position.[16] Such thoughts were never mere "theory" for Burke. Throughout his life, although he felt little pity for the *ongoing* distress of the poor, he nevertheless was deeply moved by the acute distress of those from better stations in life.[17] Sometimes Burke's responses were admirable, as when he took the unpopular position of pleading for leniency in the harsh punishment ordered for a young officer convicted of homosexuality; sometimes they showed him at his worst, as when he pleaded for funds to buy new finery for emigré French clerics. Burke was outraged by the fact that, with shabby clothes, these worthies were not being treated with the deference due them by the common people in London.[18]

The Parisot case must thus have struck Burke with real force, especially given the bond of friendship and the role women had always played in his aesthetics. It is *this* scene of distress that most likely called forth the thoughts that became part of his famous response to the royal family's seizure in October: "We are so made as to be affected at such spectacles with melancholy sentiments upon the unstable condition of mortal prosperity. . . . In those natural feelings we learn great lessons. . . . In events like these our passions instruct our reason."[19] Clearly Burke hoped his readers would be so instructed by his colorful description of the events at Versailles. But his own instruction, I am suggesting, took place before those events. In other words, in this case the provincial theater's performance was the original; the Parisian one merely a repeat, however more lavish the production.

Think how the events in Auxerre were likely to have struck Burke. As his letter in August had indicated, he was at that point weighing the possibility that the revolution would become the accelerating vehicle of political modernity. And the possibility of that acceleration was dependent upon the degree to which traditional institutions could or could not continue to evoke a sense of the sublime. As his metaphor of the aged parent and the child physician had illustrated in the early 1780s, this politically relevant or "authentic" sublime had to contain a blend of awe and affection. It is hard not to think of the Parisot letter as bringing Burke to clarity on the issue of whether the French still retained a "fund of natural moderation." The letter recounts how all order and tradition were being swept aside in that region during the Great Fear. Clearly there was no awe left in regard to established institutions. And just as obviously there was no affection. This fact was crystallized by the experience of the Parisot women. Burke probably imagined their distress being repeated throughout the countryside. If the French could not be restrained by the specific distress of *women* within the social hierarchy, how could one expect them to exhibit solicitude for any other aspect of the traditional order? Burke now knew that he was to see the full force of political modernity explode into history.

The claim that Burke saw all this in one letter may sound a bit melodramatic.[20] But his reaction is, as I have shown, amply grounded in his aesthetic perspective. Moreover the harshness of his judgment at this point is not perhaps as unreasonable as it may seem at first glance. At least one leading contemporary scholar of the revolution, referring to the political logic animating the Great Fear, has concluded, "The Terror was merely 1789 with a higher body count."[21]

If Burke's thinking is reconstructed in this fashion, it helps one to see how his decision to oppose the revolution is deeply compatible with his earlier, systematic reflections on aesthetics and political modernity. When one focuses instead, as is usually the case, on the more famous scene of Marie Antoinette's distress, this continuity becomes overshadowed by the hyperbole and histrionics of Burke's description of that event.[22] He casts her almost as an unearthly vision: There "surely never lighted on this orb, which she hardly seemed to touch, a more delightful vision." This image is juxtaposed to ones of "unutterable abominations" and "mutilated carcasses" as the king and queen are dragged from the palace and subjected to the "slow torture" of insult and degradation on the journey to Paris. The description is crowned by Burke's cloying lament:

> Little did I dream that I should have lived to see such disasters fallen upon her in a nation of gallant men, in a nation of men of honour and of cavaliers. I thought ten thousand swords must have leaped from their scabbards to avenge even a look that threatened her with insult.—But the age of chivalry is gone.[23]

These pages of the *Reflections* make it quite easy to imagine, as many have, that the Burke who confronted the revolution was a man whose judgment was in some serious way losing its moorings. This kind of interpretation is easy to slide into, given the undeniable fact that in 1789 Burke was in many ways a deeply bitter and disappointed man—in bad financial condition, often laughed at rather than respected by the younger members of Parliament, and all too aware that his crusade to impeach Hastings was doomed to failure.[24]

Burke is to a degree his own worst enemy here. He claims to have shed tears when penning his description of the queen. Moreover, he was duly warned before publication that his portrayal was likely to encounter ridicule. Philip Francis, a man with whom he worked intimately on the impeachment, had informed him bluntly after reading the manuscript of this section of the *Reflections,* "All you say of the Queen is pure foppery."[25]

Even if one ignores the Parisot letter, as is usually done, and attends only to the gilded picture of the queen, it is necessary to emphasize that there is still some clever method to this foppery. Burke's primary audience in the *Reflections* was the aristocracy and gentry of England; they would have to be a prime bulwark against the engine of revolution. The appeal to chivalry was aimed at the "second nature" of these classes. For this audience, such an appeal had a familiar ring within the traditions of English political discourse. As J.G.A. Pocock has pointed out, there was an established line of thought asserting that contemporary English political culture was superior to ancient republicanism, because the manners engendered by chivalry had modified the harsher, more austere qualities associated with the classical model of virtue.[26] Burke is thus challenging the ruling classes of England: Respond appropriately to the distress of the French queen or admit that chivalry is dead *and* that your prominent place on the stage of Western political culture is thereby forfeited!

Thus the apparently witless fop reveals himself once again to be a clever master of the language games embedded in English political traditions. The richness and continuity of Burke's thinking is enhanced even more, however, if we decenter somewhat the events at Versailles, as I suggest occurs when those in Auxerre are given the role they warrant. The appeal to chivalry then becomes not only a move within the language game just mentioned, but also a move within the language games of Burke's aesthetics and his scenario of political modernity. As I have said, the events in Auxerre convinced Burke that France could no longer draw upon that natural "fund" of the authentic sublime to support a stable order. If that fund had remained, then "pity" would have been elicited from such scenes of distress, and actions to relieve the suffering would naturally have followed. No such natural brake on the momentum of revolution seemed to be working. Revolutionary violence seemed to breed only further energy and enthusiasm. Burke therefore turns to chivalry as a possible resource of "second nature" that may still be capable of slowing the momentum, at least in England. Of course, it is unlikely that Burke thought that this would be effective by itself. The portrait of Marie Antoinette is after all only a small segment of a large text. Far more space is given over to the broader and more diffuse problem of reviving the attenuated sense of the authentic sublime in the English people through glowing descriptions of ancient institutions, whose slow maturation has solidified their freedom. The aged parent thus rises before our eyes. And Burke desperately hopes that renewed awe and solicitude will similarly emerge as the corresponding affective response.

II. Revolutionizing the Sentiments

Burke is a careful student of the multidimensionality of the French Revolution. He attends closely to the upheavals in property relations, political structures, religion, social relations, and financial institutions. But he leaves no doubt which of these "revolutions" within the revolution is at the heart of the matter: "the most important of all . . . I mean a revolution in sentiments, manners and moral opinions."[27] For Burke, our explicit moral opinions are largely structured by our manners—in the broad sense of mores—with these in turn cohering around our basic sentiments. And sentiments are called forth and cultivated from a natural aesthetic-affective soil. But this soil is, in Burke's mind, now being depleted. Traditional arrangements and institutions are no longer evoking an experience of sublimity that can be counted upon as a natural brake on social change.

Whether in France or in England, early in the 1780s this process of depletion always had, in Burke's mind, a somewhat mysterious character to it. He vacillated between despair at its providential inevitability and hope that human action could somehow reverse the process. But about one thing he was certain. The revolutionary regime in France was doing everything it could to hasten this depletion. It is this concern that explains why Burke refers so often to the theater, both metaphorically and literally, in his writings on the revolution. As noted in the preceding chapter, he had always thought of the theater as an important school for the sentiments. This view is repeated forcefully in the *Reflections*: "The theater is a better school of moral sentiments than churches."[28] Moreover, during the course of his political career, Burke had become increasingly aware that the state itself had a theatrical role in this regard. What he had never imagined is how powerfully and systematically both of these vehicles—the theater in the state and the theater of the state—might be employed. The latter harbored what was for Burke the ultimate nightmare. The state-sponsored, choreographed spectacles that became such a distinctive characteristic of the revolution showed him that the natural aesthetic-affective soil could not only be depleted, but also actively contaminated. The authentic sublime was being consciously replaced by a false one. The grotesque imagery that is so prominent in Burke's writing on France has its basis in these worries. He was imagining the full development of the profuse jungle of mutant vegetation that was already beginning to sprout from the contaminated soil.

The chaos Burke saw in France might thus be categorized in terms of two types of theater and their effects on aesthetic-affective dynamics: the theater of depletion and the theater of regeneration.

The Theater of Depletion. By 1790, Burke had no doubt that a tragedy was taking place in what he later called "the moral theater of the world."[29] But the action on the Paris stage was so infused with spectacle, buffoonery, grotesqueness, and chaos that the true nature of the play was not evident.

Thus, at the beginning of the *Reflections,* Burke refers to this "monstrous tragicomic scene" where "the most opposite passions necessarily succeed and sometimes mix with each other in the mind: alternate contempt and indignation, alternate laughter and tears, alternate scorn and horror."[30]

This description of French politics is no offhand derisory slap. For one thing, a continuity of imagery is maintained up through Burke's last works.[31] More important, though, tragicomedy has a distinct aesthetic significance for him. It constituted the systematic debasement of tragedy. Tragic drama, as he stated many years earlier, is a medium in which the passions and attitudes associated with the sublime should hold sway: "admiration, terror, pity," and a sense of humility in the face of mortality.[32] This understanding of tragedy is what guides his literary reenactment of the Versailles seizure: the evocation of admiration and pity for the royal family; of terror at the revolutionary violence; and finally of "melancholy sentiments" tied to a realization of "the unstable condition of mortal prosperity, and the tremendous uncertainty of human greatness."[33]

When Burke refers to tragicomedy, he is speaking not so much of a coherent type of drama as of a debasement of tragedy that can assume a variety of forms. He had first seen one form of this phenomenon as a young man in Dublin. In an issue of *The Reformer,* Burke excoriated a production of *Macbeth* that had been amended with healthy doses of buffoonery and lewdness.[34] Just as he attacked this Dublin troupe of players for obfuscating the aesthetic-affective dynamics of Shakespeare's tragedy, so Burke in 1790 attacks the leaders of the revolution for obfuscating the tragedy of France.

For the form and passions of tragedy, tragicomedy substitutes anything that can titillate and entertain. The actors aim at a virtuosity of transgression, a loosening up of all bonds restraining the human will and passions.[35] In this vein Burke speaks in 1790 of the National Assembly as acting "like the comedians of a fair before a riotous audience."[36] What he sees emerging is a reciprocal incitement of revolutionary actor and audience that rapidly depletes the natural sensibility for the authentic sublime. The end point of this theatrical downward spiral is painted in vivid colors in his "Letters on a Regicide Peace." After remarking that he has it on good authority that the space underneath the guillotine's bloody scaffold "was hired out for a show of dancing dogs," he offers the following description of Parisian life. It is like "a lewd tavern for the revels and debauches of banditti, assassins, bravos, smugglers, and their more desperate paramours, mixed with bombastick players, the refuse and rejected offal of strolling theatres, puffing out ill-sorted verses about virtue, mixed with . . . licentious and blasphemous songs."[37] This is Burke at his hyperbolic best (or worst). But even he cannot imagine that something of such magnitude has been achieved by the debased performances of a few revolutionary leaders on the stage of the National Assembly. The theaters of Paris bear a heavy burden of blame in their own right in this revolution of the sentiments.

Burke draws a sharp contrast between the suppression of churches and courts of law, on the one hand, and the explosion in the number of theaters in the French capital, on the other. He sees these new theaters as tools of the revolution, their debased repertoire mirroring that of the political leadership.[38] During the Terror, some of these theaters were indeed supported by public money and under strict revolutionary censorship. But to focus on this specific aspect of control is to miss the underlying issue that animates Burke. His concern is more like that of contemporary critics of U.S. television who worry about the effects of its intense commercialism and violence on a population whose members reportedly spend over forty hours a week in front of their sets. Although this comparison might sound far fetched, it becomes less so when one realizes the extraordinary salience of theater in revolutionary Paris. Consider the following description in a standard history of French theater at this time:

A statistician of the times calculated that twenty-three . . . theatres opened in Paris [in 1791] and that their total seating capacity added to the others required 60,000 persons daily to attend the theatre for all to support themselves. The population of Paris in 1791 was about 650,000. "If this goes on," one critic complained, "Paris will have a theatre in every street, an actor in every house, a musician in every basement, and an author in every garret."[39]

Burke was quite fearful that this same cultural phenomenon would spread to Britain. He turns to this topic in his last extended piece of writing, the "Third Letter on a Regicide Peace," which was published a few months after his death in 1797.[40] The main goal in this letter, as in the preceding ones, is to convince the British government that it should not make peace with revolutionary France. In this final letter, he tries to demonstrate that the war has not brought about any impoverishment of Britain; on the contrary, commerce is flourishing. Among a mass of tables dealing with the

trade in tea, furs, glass plate, and so forth, Burke pauses to ponder the
recent increase in theaters throughout the country. He is quick to warn
against the "new style" that seems to be emerging of "gaudy and pompous
entertainments." This is precisely the soil into which the "principles of
Jacobinism enter."[41]

The Theater of Regeneration. Thus what Burke gathers under the rubric
of tragicomedy—whether it occurs in the National Assembly or the play-
houses—are phenomena of depletion and degeneration. This is only one
side, however, of the underlying revolution in France. The other aesthetic-
affective side of the "modern system of morality and policy" is a theater
of regeneration that promises infinite resources of energy and will for the
revolutionary cause. Accordingly, when Burke asserts that Jacobin "morality
has no idea in it of restraint," he is not just referring to its destruction of
all the social, political, and religious limits embedded in traditional societies,
but also to its making limitlessness its innermost principle of animation.[42]

At the time Burke first used the metaphor of the aged parent, he contrasted the proper role of the wise child physician with that of a magician
trying to restore the patient to "youth and vigor." This magician is cast as
a somewhat ludicrous figure: to be feared, but also exposed and laughed
at. When Burke employs the metaphor again in the context of the *Reflections,* there is still the mixture of ludicrousness and fear; but the fear from
this point on becomes far stronger. For the metaphysical magicians of France
just might be successful; out of their new science may emerge a powerfully
energetic creature, a "new species": "The moral world admits of Monsters
which the physical rejects."[43] Here one sees emerging vividly, and perhaps
for the first time, the moral cousin of that physical monster of the modern
imaginary: Frankenstein.[44]

This revolutionary being is nourished in a new aesthetic-affective soil.
Sublimity, as Burke has understood it up to this point, is an experience of
terrible delight producing in turn a soberness and humility that reflects a
vivified sense of human finitude. What he has to admit now is that this
sense of the sublime—which he sees as authentic—is being rapidly sup-
planted by one that is radically different. A new second nature is being
created that does not gently modify first nature, but rather goes "all the
way down" and eradicates it.

A short time after the seizure at Versailles in October 1789, Burke read
a copy of a sermon given by the Reverend Richard Price, a dissenting

minister, to a group in London called the Revolution Society. Price extolled the French Revolution and asserted that it was bringing to fruition radical political principles, the seeds of which the English had first planted when they toppled James II in the Glorious Revolution of 1688. Burke was outraged both by Price's enthusiastic reception of events in France and his attempt to harmonize its principles with those of English political traditions. The first section of the *Reflections* is an extended response to Price.[45] The intensity of Burke's feelings on this matter arose from the fact that Price and his associates represented a frightening glimpse of what might happen soon to the broader population in England, the danger of what he came to call English Jacobinism. In his response, Burke tries to dislodge Price's reading of history; more specifically, he redraws the lines of revolutionary filiation. The lineage of Price and his French allies extends back not to the Glorious Revolution of 1688, but rather to the darker era of the English Civil War of 1640. The political connotations evoked for Burke's contemporaries thus shifted from positive to negative: to the tyranny of Oliver Cromwell.[46]

In aesthetic-affective terms, this shift allows Burke to make the revolutionaries of his own day the heirs to that dangerous and familiar disease of religious fanaticism or "enthusiasm."[47] This in turn puts a more disturbing face on the "exultation and rapture" manifested by Price and his ilk in the face of the drama in France.[48] To awaken these associations even further, Burke casts Price in the role of Hugh Peters, the Calvinist minister who spoke at the execution of Charles I in 1649. Burke's overall purpose is abundantly evident; Price and his friends, like the Calvinists of the preceding century, claim a privileged source of inspiration that trumps all traditional institutions; and if they are not suppressed, they will usher in a frenzy of destruction.

However much Burke attempted to brand his English opponents with this kind of stigma, he knew in his own mind that the Jacobin spirit harbored novel dangers. For one thing, even when comparing the revolutionary regime in France to that of Cromwell, he makes it clear that the latter, once in power, cared more for establishing order than promoting religious zeal.[49] For the former, however, the attainment of power merely provides a more effective place from which to accelerate the revolution. This new species is engaged in "an industry without limit."[50]

The parallel between Cromwell and the French likely suggested early on to Burke that the probable fate of Louis XVI would be execution. But again the parallel only carries so far. Charles I had indeed ultimately been executed; but beforehand he never became a mere player in an ongoing revolutionary spectacle, as did Louis. In this regard, it is interesting to see what Burke has to say about the great festival held in Paris on July 14, 1790, the first anniversary of the fall of the Bastille. I will have more to say below about the general significance of such revolutionary fêtes. For the moment, one need only consider Burke's judgment concerning this anniversary, during which the king and queen were forced to play scripted roles in a monumental revolutionary show. The Fête de la Fédération involved several hundred thousand people gathered in a vast amphitheater in the Champs de Mars, in the center of which stood the "Altar of the Fatherland" for revolutionary leaders and the royal family. Of this scene, Burke offers the following startling observation: "The horrors of the 5th and 6th of October [the Versailles seizure] were *less detestable* than the festival of the 14th of July."[51]

What explains this extraordinary judgment? However horrible, the events in October resembled a street fair turned riot: passions unleashed, violence, and disorder. These things were detestable, and the evidence they gave of a depletion of the natural fund of aesthetic-affective moderation was frightening. But in a way they paled in significance when compared with the fête of the following July. This is because the latter crystallized the true aesthetic-affective innovation of the revolution: the false sublime.[52]

Burke's critique of the revolution is often largely associated with his attacks on abstract, rationalist ideas hatched in the "cold" hearts of metaphysicians and atheists. But on their own, these are hardly the stuff of revolution, especially for someone who saw passions as so often more powerful motives for action than reason or interest.[53] One senses Burke's awareness of this problem, and senses as well the inadequacy of his comparison of the spirit animating France with the religious enthusiasm of the English Civil War, when he writes: "Who could have imagined that Atheism could have produced one of the most violently operative principles of fanaticism?"[54] Something more therefore has to be supplied to construct an explanation of the revolution that fits Burke's own understanding of human motivation and social interaction.

The fête of July 1790 constituted for Burke only the most egregious manifestation of the emergence of a new aesthetic-affective dynamic. A regenerated, but radically different, sublime was in circulation. One might characterize this phenomenon as a "humanization" of the sublime. This term has been used to denote a certain tendency in how the sublime began to be rethought in nineteenth- and twentieth-century art and literature.[55] Humanization in this sense means that the object of sublime experience is increasingly associated with feats of human subjectivity; for example, those of the genius in the eyes of the romantics, or those of the avant-garde artist who is out to shock her audience. Human beings themselves now *produce* a sort of *human infinite* that displaces what had before stood for the infinite, God, or fate.

I want to suggest that Burke saw such a phenomenon already in the eighteenth century, and he understood it to be a crucial component of a new sort of tyranny. The concept of tyranny as Burke and others had used it up to this point implied, of course, a kind of illegitimate willfulness in the use of power. But this willfulness, however aggressive, was always tied to particular persons and objects. In revolutionary France, this changes: A false sublime now allows the familiar vice of "vanity" to cathect itself to the unlimited horizons of rational imagination.[56] With this, human will becomes empowered not simply to transgress specific limits, but rather to embrace limitlessness itself. And once this animating principle installs itself in politics, any given obstacle to a regime's will becomes merely an object to annihilate. Well in advance of the Terror, Burke grasped the logic of such a system: "At the end of every visto, you see nothing but the gallows." Only later did others come to a similar realization. This insight is perhaps most powerfully captured in an engraving done after Robespierre's fall. It shows the leader of the Terror standing before a forest of guillotines, guillotining the executioner, the only other person left alive in France.[57]

The taste for a humanized sublime received its most visible enhancement through the medium of vast public spectacles staged to generate loyalty to the revolution. Although as I have shown, Burke often derided the revolution's leaders as bad tragicomic actors, he nevertheless feared their virtuosity in this novel mode of public theater. Included within its domain were such things as the elaborately staged public funerals of revolutionary heroes, masterminded by the arch impresario of the revolution, Jacques-Louis David, as well as the "traveling revolution kit" of Patriot Palloy, who toured the provinces and reenacted the fall of the Bastille. During the months Burke was working on the *Reflections,* what most likely caught his attention, though, were the fêtes held by the revolutionary federations. The

one in Paris in July 1790 was merely the largest of a series that took place
throughout France from the end of 1789 to summer 1790. These spectacles
often involved tens of thousands of participants. Their flavor can be gained
from a description of the one held in Strasbourg. There,

> The Federation of the Rhine assembled fifty thousand guardsmen from all
> over eastern France, from the Haute-Marne to the Jura. Thousands more ci-
> vilians were used as ceremonial extras, all heavily clad in the wardrobe of
> revolutionary religiosity. Four hundred adolescent girls dressed in virginal
> white bobbed up and down on the river Ill in a flotilla of tricolor-painted
> boats before proceeding to a huge "patriotic altar" erected on the Plaine des
> Bouchers. Two hundred small children were ritually adopted by National
> Guardsmen as the "future of the *patrie*"; fishermen dedicated the Rhine and
> its fish to the cause of freedom. Patriotic farmers were preceded in parade by
> plows pushed by intergenerational teams of children and old men all carrying
> sickles and scythes. Most important of all was the symbolism of confessional
> unity as two toddlers, one Protestant, one Catholic (in a city with a strong
> Reformation presence), were subjected to an ecumenical baptism with shared
> godparents of both faiths. Their new names were declared to be "Fédéré" and
> "Civique."[58]

Burke sees quite clearly how crucial such "grand spectacle" is to the
stoking of revolutionary fires: "The marvelous must be produced." In earlier ages, he writes, marvels were associated with the supernatural; in the
enlightened, modern world this connection is no longer convincing. The
marvelous must be brought down to earth and consciously constructed out
of novelty and surprise. The awe and wonder traditionally associated with
what is *beyond* life now becomes astonishment and titillation at the "marvelous *in* life, in manners, in characters, and in extraordinary situations"
(my emphasis).[59]

The French themselves, of course, thought they were merely reviving
the exultation and energy associated with the classical sublime. In this
sense, they imagined themselves in the role of the sons in David's immensely influential painting, *The Oath of the Horatii.* There the Roman
sons with outstretched arms take a patriotic oath before their father. This
gesture of the arm soon became the accepted form for swearing revolutionary allegiance, just as many other symbols were borrowed from republican
Rome for use during the revolution.

For Burke, however, this neoclassical veneer obscured a radical shift.
One way to understand this shift is to reconsider a point in Longinus's *On*

the Sublime. Speaking of the effect on the hearer of a sublime poem or speech, he writes, "Our soul is uplifted . . . and is filled with joy and vaunting, *as though* it had itself produced what it has heard."[60] I think it is fair to say that Longinus would extend his insight to all experiences of the sublime. What is interesting in the present context is the way in which this thought allows one to locate the radical break effected by the aesthetics of the French Revolution. As I said earlier, in the classical sublime—as well as Burke's—one undergoes an experience born out of a momentary interface of limits and limitlessness. The limited self feels the existence of what is in some sense beyond limits. In this there is a vicarious participation: the subject's feeling of delight, "as though" it is what produced the object of the experience.

Now what separates this from the modern, false sublime is the latter's dissolution of the "as though." The self and the social collective no longer participate vicariously, but rather refigure themselves as the permanent embodiment of infinitude. The revolutionary fete was both a mirror and an accelerator of this new self-conception. The sublime was, as it were, brought down to earth and made available systematically. With this transformation or humanization of the sublime, all radical otherness, all that is beyond familiar limits—be it divine, natural, or human—is leveled out, leaving only wide open vistas for modern projects.

Thus a distorted, humanized sublime is a constitutive feature of the modern revolutionary consciousness exploding onto the historical stage in France. Burke is torn between his fear of all this as inevitable and his desperate hope that he can still enlist the forces necessary to stamp it out. Accordingly, his language of analysis regarding the false sublime vacillates between an epochal tone and a scornful, deprecating one. He asks at one point in the *Reflections* what holds the revolutionary state together. His answer is that it is nothing more than the army and the paper money speculations of the National Assembly, neither of which will be effective in the long run. He speaks dismissively in this context of the revolutionaries' "confederations, their *spectacles,* their civic feasts, and their enthusiasm": These are "mere tricks."[61] Of course, the false sublime does represent a kind of trickery in the sense of willful, systematic artifice that Burke thinks is deceptive. It is difficult, however, to take literally the other sense Burke has in mind here: something to be taken lightly. He takes this no more lightly than the metaphysical magician's efforts to conjure up a new parental constitution.

One should remember in this regard Burke's remark about the counterrevolutionary army he hoped would be formed to invade France. It had to be one in which none of the soldiers spoke French. Evidently Burke worried that they might be animated by something more than mere trickery.

III. The Authentic Sublime

Even if Burke ultimately was unsure about the possibility of stopping the tide of political modernity, he nevertheless campaigned tirelessly in the last years of his life for the military eradication of the revolutionary regime in France, as well as for the suppression of what he felt were its subversive sympathizers within his own country. The latter could not be allowed to contaminate any further the already depleted aesthetic-affective soil of England. In this ardent appeal to force for the purpose of preserving the hold of an authentic sublime, however, Burke maneuvers himself into a position against which his own charge of mere trickery gains ironic resonance. This difficulty can be grasped by considering his response to an event that took place shortly before he died. It was one of the last public problems on which he commented. A mutiny had broken out in the British navy in spring 1797. Sailors of the Channel Fleet at Spithead simply refused to obey orders until their pay was increased. The government was disposed to negotiate a resolution, and within a month an increase was granted. Burke fumed against this course of action, which he felt was too conciliatory. Rather than send a negotiator to the mutineers, he thought "a great Naval commander" should have been dispatched "to awe the seditious into obedience."[62]

This outburst presents in microcosm the impasse at which Burke's aesthetic and political reflections finally leave us. All around him in 1797, traditional structures of authority are being brought into question. What is to be done? Back in the 1770s and early 1780s, Burke could perhaps still think of a process by which the people and government reciprocally contribute to the cultivation of a renewed sense of the sublime. But that time is past. Cultivation of any sort is always a slow process, and the danger of political modernity is now overwhelming. Burke's response in this situation is to recommend a kind of aesthetic trickery: instant, "official theater" to shore up the status quo. And if the audience of sailors had not reacted appropriately, it seems clear that Burke would have recommended violent suppression.

The reflections Burke had developed over a lifetime on the significance of the authentic sublime for a legitimate political order thus come to a pretty disreputable end: the image of a theater production whose audience is surrounded by an armed force and applauds on cue. The sublime here has in effect become just as much a political management tool as it was in France. These tools perhaps can still be distinguished, but now only by the different evils they entail for politics in the modern world. Thus Burke may be immensely perceptive in his analysis of a false sublime, but he may also be guilty of exactly the charges leveled at him by contemporaries like Tom Paine and Mary Wollstonecraft, who argued that his aesthetics reduced to nothing more than an attempt to bamboozle the common people.[63] Whether in regard to the specific demands of the sailors or the broader ones for individual rights and a popular voice in political life, Burke's political aesthetics seems to be fleshed out as injustice with plumage. If there is any latent wisdom here, it will have to be drawn out by reading him at least somewhat against the grain.

Notes

1. The most skillful attempt to identify how various language games common to eighteenth-century British political thought structure the argument of the *Reflections* comes from J. G. A. Pocock. See his "Introduction" in *Reflections on the Revolution in France* (Indianapolis: Hackett, 1987), pp. vii-xiviii; the essays in *Virtue, Commerce and History* (Cambridge: Cambridge University Press, 1985); "Burke and the Ancient Constitution," in *Politics, Language and Time* (New York: Atheneum, 1971), pp. 202-32; and "Edmund Burke and the Redefinition of Enthusiasm: The Context as Counter-Revolution," in *The French Revolution and the Creation of Modern Political Culture*, Vol. 3, *The Transformation of Political Culture 1789-1848*, ed. F. Furet & M. Ozouf (Oxford, U.K.: Pergamon, 1989), pp. 19-35.

2. Conor Cruise O'Brien, *The Great Melody: A Thematic Biography* (Chicago: University of Chicago, 1992), pp. ixx-ixxiii, 457.

3. See especially, *Corr.*, VIII, p. 254.

4. *Corr.*, VIII, p. 129.

5. See "Letter to the Sheriffs of Bristol," *Works*, II, p. 244; "Address to the King," *Works*, VI, p. 165; "Thoughts on the Present Discontents," *WS*, II, p. 258; "Speech on Representation," *Works*, VII, p. 95.

6. *Reflections on the Revolution in France*, *WS*, VIII, p. 313.

7. Ibid., p. 137. Cf. "Speech on Representation," *Works,* VII, pp. 93-96.

8. *Corr.,* VI, p. 10. My emphasis.

9. Alfred Cobban and Robert A. Smith, the editors of volume VI of *The Correspondence of Edmund Burke,* interpret his remark about having seen "something like it in progress of several years" as referring broadly to "the financial difficulties of France;" *Corr.,* VI, p. 10, n. 2. This seems to be a curious reading, given the specific sense of the paragraph at issue, with its reference to the dynamics of revolutionary violence. My suggestion that it was the Gordon Riots that were on Burke's mind in this letter coincides to a degree with O'Brien's view that the riots played an important role in Burke's interpretation of the French Revolution. O'Brien, however, emphasizes only the theme of anti-Catholicism common to the upheavals of 1782 and 1789; *The Great Melody,* pp. 395-96. My interpretation also fits with Burke's own later assertion that the spirit of Jacobinism arose *first* in England; see Chapter 1, p. 15.

10. "Appeal From the New to the Old Whigs," *Works,* IV, p. 192.

11. The fact that Burke is still ambivalent *after* the constitutional changes of the summer would appear to indicate that these changes alone did not induce him to turn "decisively" against the revolution. This claim has been put forward recently by Michael Mosher, "The Skeptic's Burke: *Reflections on the Revolution in France, 1790-1990,*" *Political Theory* 19 (August 1991): 401-2.

12. Letter from Madame Parisot to Richard Burke, Jr., *Corr.,* VI, pp. 16-17.

13. *Corr.,* VI, p. 25.

14. Recent examples of scholars who accord this letter pivotal status are O'Brien, *The Great Melody,* p. 388; and Mosher, "The Skeptic's Burke," pp. 401-2.

15. *Corr.,* VI, p. 26.

16. *Inquiry, Works,* I, pp. 118-19, 243.

17. Cf. the remark by the salon hostess Mrs. Crewe that: "Those who had known luxury and were reduced met with most of his compassion." Quoted in Stanley Ayling, *Edmund Burke: His Life and Opinions* (New York: St. Martin's, 1988), p. 139.

18. *Corr.,* IV, pp. 230, 402; *Corr.,* VII, p. 226; and "Letter to the National Assembly", *WS,* VIII, p. 304.

19. *Reflections, WS,* VIII, p. 131.

20. The only contemporary scholar I am aware of who mentions this letter does so disparagingly; that is, merely to give a flavor of the sort of "highly colored" evidence Burke drew upon in forming his judgments about the revolution. See L. G. Mitchell, "Introduction," in *WS,* VIII, p. 3.

21. Simon Schama, *Citizens: A Chronicle of the French Revolution* (New York: Vintage, 1989), pp. 431-46, 437. My point here is not to claim that either Burke or Schama is necessarily correct, rather only that Burke's judgment here is not simply idiosyncratic.

22. J. T. Boulton calls the apostrophe to Marie Antoinette the "centerpiece of the *Reflections*"; *The Language of Politics in the Age of Wilkes and Burke* (London: Routledge, 1963) p. 98.

23. *Reflections, WS,* VIII, pp. 121-27.

24. Cf., for example, F. P. Lock's judgment that "the *Reflections* is the book of an embittered man writing in near-despair"; *Burke's Reflections on the Revolution in France* (London: Allen & Unwin, 1985), p. 31.

25. *Corr.,* VI, pp. 85-92.

26. J. G. A. Pocock, "The Political Economy of Burke's Analysis of the French Revolution," in *Virtue, Commerce, and History,* pp. 193-212.

27. *Reflections, WS,* VIII, p. 131.

28. Ibid., p. 132.

29. "First Letter on a Regicide Peace," *WS,* IX, p. 188.

30. *Reflections, WS,* VIII, p. 60.

31. "Fourth Letter on a Regicide Peace," *WS,* IX, p. 77.

32. "Hints for an Essay on the Drama," *Works,* VII, p. 150.

33. *Reflections, WS,* VIII, p. 131.

34. See the discussion in Paul Hindson and Tim Gray, *Burke's Dramatic Theory of Politics* (Aldershot, U.K.: Avebury, 1988), pp. 131-32.

35. Cf. Ibid., p. 138.

36. *Reflections, WS,* VIII, p. 119.

37. "First Letter on a Regicide Peace," *WS,* IX, pp. 246-47.

38. Ibid., p. 246; "Fourth Letter on a Regicide Peace," *WS,* IX, p. 114.

39. Martin Carlson, *The Theater of the French Revolution* (Ithaca, NY: Cornell University Press, 1966), p. 111. I have corrected a misprint in Carlson. The text has "65,000"; it should be 650,000.

40. Although there were four of these letters, the third was actually written last.

41. "Third Letter on a Regicide Peace," *WS,* IX, p. 370.

42. *Corr.,* VI, p. 210.

43. "Third Letter on a Regicide Peace," *WS,* IX, p. 358; and "Fourth Letter on a Regicide Peace," *WS,* IX, p. 96.

44. Mary Shelley published *Frankenstein, or the Modern Prometheus* in 1818.

45. *Reflections, WS,* VIII, pp. 54-114.

46. Ibid., pp. 61-63, 66-67.

47. J.G.A. Pocock has been the most prominent supporter of the argument that Burke wanted his English contemporaries to see the French Revolution not as something new, but as a religious-political phenomenon they had already seen. Thus, he says, the revolution was, for Burke, "primarily an event in the religious history of Europe." But Pocock is also aware that this effort to contextualize the revolution was not ultimately persuasive for Burke himself. The horror of the revolution rather finally resides in its radical newness. Pocock interprets this moment in Burke's thought as follows: "The revolutionary force which Burke struggles to diagnose is that of the irrational; of words and deeds restrained and rendered intelligible by no context." My suggestion is that we best capture this moment of radicality not with labels like "irrational" but with a further context Pocock neglects: the language of aesthetics. Pocock, "Edmund Burke and the Redefinition of Enthusiasm," in *The French Revolution and the Creation of Political Culture,* ed. Furet & Ozouf, pp. 27, 34.

48. *Reflections, WS,* VIII, p. 60.

49. "Remarks on the Policy of the Allies" (1793), *WS,* VIII, pp. 497-98.

50. *Reflections,* quoted in Peter H. Melvin, "Burke on Theatricality and Revolution," *Journal of the History of Ideas* 36 (1975): 459.

51. "Letter to the National Assembly," *WS,* VIII, pp. 309-10. My emphasis.

52. Although Burke did not use the term "false sublime," it is my claim that he develops such a conception and that the term would not have appeared strange to him. Interestingly, J. T. Boulton, the most careful interpreter of the *Inquiry* in the twentieth century, suggests that Burke may indeed have actually used the term. The occurrence is in an anonymous letter that Boulton attributes to Burke; see "Editor's Introduction," in Edmund Burke, *A Philosophical Enquiry Into the Origin of Our Ideas of the Sublime and Beautiful,* ed. with introduction and notes by J. T. Boulton (New York: Columbia University Press, 1958), pp. cxii-xciii. There have been other attempts to discern some notion of a false sublime in Burke. See Ian Hampsher-Monk,

"Rhetoric and Opinion in the Politics of Edmund Burke," *History of Political Thought* 9 (Winter 1988): 482-83; and W.J.T. Mitchell, "Eye and Ear: Edmund Burke and the Politics of Sensibility," in *Iconology: Image, Text, Ideology* (Chicago: University of Chicago Press, 1986), pp. 125-49, especially p. 132. See also the reference to Paulson in note 55 below.

53. Cf. "First Letter on a Regicide Peace," *WS*, IX, p. 247.

54. "Remarks on the Policy of the Allies," *WS*, VIII, p. 499.

55. Ronald Paulson, "Versions of a Human Sublime," in *New Literary History* (Special issue on the sublime) 16 (1985): 427-37. In an earlier book on the aesthetics of the French Revolution, Paulson suggests the notion of a "false sublime," but quickly drops it without tying it to the issue of the humanization of the sublime; *Representations of Revolution 1789-1820* (New Haven, CT: Yale University Press, 1983) p. 66.

56. On "vanity," see "Letter to the National Assembly," *WS*, VIII, pp. 313-14.

57. *Reflections, WS*, VIII, p. 128. For a reproduction of the engraving, see Schama, *Citizens*, p. 850.

58. Ibid., pp. 409-19, 503, 671-73, 741-45. These revolutionary spectacles continued, of course, after the one in July 1990 in Paris. The most infamous of these was Robespierre's Festival of the Supreme Being.

59. *Reflections, WS*, VIII, p. 219. Cf. Frans de Bruyn, "Hooking the Leviathan: The Eclipse of the Heroic and the Emergence of the Sublime in Eighteenth Century British Literature," *The Eighteenth Century: Theory and Interpretation* 28 (Winter 1987): 210. My emphasis.

60. Longinus, quoted in Thomas Weiskel, *The Romantic Sublime* (Baltimore, MD: Johns Hopkins University Press, 1976), p. 3. My emphasis.

61. *Reflections, WS*, VIII, p. 167.

62. *Corr.*, IX, pp. 347-48.

63. Tom Paine, "The Rights of Man," in *Paine: Political Writings,* ed. Bruce Kuklick (Cambridge: Cambridge University Press, 1989); and Mary Wollstonecraft, *A Vindication of the Rights of Men* (Delmar, NY: Scholar's Facsimiles and Reprints, 1975).

5

Conclusion

In this book, I have tried to make the case that Burke's aesthetic reflections are crucial to a full understanding of his political reflections. In conclusion, I want to try to make a more speculative claim, namely, that the aesthetics will also help one separate the wisdom in Burke's work from its reactionary excesses and blindness.

The preliminary question here is the one I raised briefly in Chapter 1. If as is usually the case, we identify Burke's wisdom with his critique of revolutionary radicalism and rationalism, then do we not have to admit that his significance as a political thinker recedes in the late twentieth century as this threat itself recedes? Revolutions no doubt will continue to occur, and they will continue to be infused with ideology. But the collapse of communism in the Soviet Union and Eastern Europe may signal the end of a distinct period of revolutions. It is hard to imagine a new revolution occurring—and being successful—with exactly the same ideological alloy that characterized both the French Revolution and the communist ones of this century: universalism; rationalism; an optimistic, secular faith in the future; and most important, a theoretical confidence in the purity of revolutionary violence. If this is true, then Burke's wisdom on these matters may be permanently important, but it will have no immediate resonance for late modern life in highly industrialized societies.

But perhaps one can reconstruct another dimension of Burke's wisdom that confronts us in a more engaging fashion. Such an approach would begin by asking whether his critique of political modernity might be permitted to count not only against "them"—revolutionaries—but also against "us." The path to this broadening of the resonance of Burke's wisdom runs through his aesthetics. I have shown how deeply his reaction to political modernity is entwined with his notion of the sublime, and more specifically, with his conviction that an authentic experience of the sublime is giving way to a false sort of experience. Further, I have elucidated how this authentic sublime is understood by Burke to be an experience that vivifies our sense of finitude, whereas the false sublime deadens it, inserting in its place a human infinitude.

When these themes are foregrounded, Burke's critique of modernity begins to exhibit some family resemblance to contemporary ones that have focused upon the costs of the modern imperatives of rationalization, especially the unlimited drive to mastery, both of the self and of the world around us. In Burke's hyperbolic language of attack and despair, one hears curious echoes of twentieth-century thinkers such as the later Heidegger, or Horkheimer and Adorno in *Dialectic of Enlightenment,* as well as of some contemporary, postmodern philosophers.[1] Huge differences, of course, remain.[2] My only point in noting these faint lines of filiation is to suggest that the problems Burke might be seen as addressing broaden significantly once we let the dangers he saw escape their confinement in explicitly revolutionary consciousness.

The initial expectation of insight generated by such a shift in focus dims rather quickly, however. As I showed at the end of the preceding chapter, Burke's explicit solution to the dangers of modernity and the false sublime slides all too easily into the dismal choreography of official theater. A reader of Burke thus must always approach his prescriptions with a high degree of ambivalence. Consider the following advice about the proper attitude that should accompany political action: "Always acting as if in the presence of canonized forefathers, the spirit of freedom, leading itself to misrule and excess, is tempered by an awful gravity."[3]

One might read this as expressing Burke's best insights about the sublime and its potential effect on our modern confidence in the efficacy of our projects. But one might also read it as Nietzsche would have. Then the "spirit of freedom" appears as weighted down by a leaden, life-deadening "spirit of gravity" (as Zarathustra calls it) carried by the state and its established church.[4] This is not awe-full, only awful.

I suspect that relatively few people today would want to embrace this leaden Burke. Renouncing him, however, does of course mean reading the historical Burke somewhat against the grain. And yet it must also be noted that Burke himself provides resources for such a rereading. His own disgust at the "managed marvels" of the French regime can be turned rather quickly upon institutional efforts to deploy "canonized forefathers" and other awe-full objects for specific purposes. In effect, Burke's own perceptiveness about the sublime and finitude undercuts his willingness to subscribe to official theater.

Burke's openness to such aesthetic management of the populace is rooted ultimately in a belief that has few contemporary adherents. This is the notion of a Great Chain of Being linking all creation in hierarchies of superiors and subordinates. Burke understood this chain as having an important link running through the human population. The broad populace occupied a position of subordination in the sense of being largely incompetent politically. The stratum of politically competent classes—the aristocracy and landed gentry—would always be required to rule them. The former have the capacity, drawn out by education and leisure, "to put moral chains upon their own appetites."[5] They may abdicate this responsibility, as did the political elites of France. But that only brings disaster, because the broad populace simply does not have an adequate capacity to "chain" itself morally. Restraint for them must come in largely political and juridical forms, that is, from *"a power out of themselves."*[6]

If today we no longer accept such a natural division between the politically competent and the politically incompetent, and thus conclude that official theater is appropriate for no one, then the issue of Burke's wisdom—or better, "latent wisdom"—takes an interesting turn. He now confronts us with the question: How does *any* individual cultivate *for herself* an authentic sense of the sublime? Institutional politics may periodically give rise to sublime moments, but the *collective* cultivation of them (from the "outside" as it were) will always engender the drift Burke captured so well in his notion of the false sublime. The marvels of human infinitude may be more blatant and extreme, such as the spectacles of Mao Zedong's

"cultural revolution" of the 1960s, or they may be more subtle and insidious, such as the campaign spectacles of U.S. presidential elections, with
their hand-picked audiences, their regulation-size flags to be waved, and
their speeches aimed primarily at capturing a few sound bites on the national news. The latter sort of phenomena are probably an inevitable part
of a society in which televisual reality penetrates everyday reality so deeply.
If so, it is especially salutary that Burke's wisdom regarding the sublime
should advise us to be intensely skeptical.

But beyond this skepticism of "managed marvels" what content might
the idea of individual cultivation of the sublime have, and what implications does it have for politics? I want to approach this question in an indirect
manner. My attempt to wrestle a wisdom out of Burke may seem somewhat less suspicious if I briefly show that a couple of other familiar read-
ings of his wisdom also cannot be drawn out effortlessly; they too must be
wrestled from the historical Burke. After a sketch of Burke "the defender
of tradition" and Burke "the fighter against injustice," I will return to a
further elaboration of an admittedly latent wisdom regarding the sublime.

Reconsider now the metaphor of the aged parent and the child physician. The aged parent stands for the traditional institutions of the polity;
the child physician is the individual citizen. Burke is often read as saying
categorically that all basic traditions must be revered and left essentially
untouched. But that reading, which derives a basic political principle from
the metaphor, simply does not sit well with many things Burke said and
did. His stands, for example, on economic reform, the slave trade, India,
and Ireland all showed a willingness to allow the claim of tradition to be
trumped sometimes.[7] His hyperbolic defense of tradition in the 1790s may
seem to allow little room for exceptions to the rule of reverence for basic
traditions; but it must always be remembered that he was responding to the
totalizing revolutionary demand for the extirpation of all political traditions. If we step back from the things he said under this polemical pressure,
then his position seems to be more one of recommending a persistent care
for, and initial humility toward, such traditions. But this would mean that
Burke leaves us with something more like a political ethos than a determi-
nate political principle or principles.

Once one begins to think of Burke in terms of such an ethos, one must
quickly admit also that the recommendations about traditions could not
constitute on their own a full description of it. One would have to include

as well some accounting of the values that he allowed to trump traditions. Most important here is the value of justice; more specifically, Burke's willingness to allow tradition to be trumped if it is entangled with substantial political injustice. In his understanding of the scheme of God's purposes, the role of the sublime is to humble us and call us back to our duties.[8] And our "first duty," Burke tells us, is to "struggle against injustice."[9] This theme has been made the leitmotif of Burke's life in a recent biography. It is the fight against tyranny (basically a liberal's fight) that constitutes the "great melody" running through his speeches and writings.[10]

But just as with the defense of tradition, a straightforward picture of Burke as a fighter against injustice is one-sided at best. Its problems are so deep that the notion of Burke as an unambiguous purveyor of a liberal political ethos along these lines is unsustainable. In the broadest sense, Burke's thinking about injustice can have little resonance today unless it is radically dissociated from its background assumptions concerning the Great Chain of Being, which allowed him to interpret as simply inevitable many things we would find to be unjust and subject to remedy.

A related, but more specific issue, however, perhaps raises in the sharpest way the reason why Burkean wisdom cannot be easily couched as a teaching about injustice. The issue could be phrased as follows: When exactly does a claim of injustice trump the presumptive claim of tradition not to be disturbed? I doubt if one can extrapolate an answer from Burke's writings that is even partially satisfactory. The reason is simply that he always remained deeply ambivalent about these matters. His ambivalence here resulted from his fear that the language of injustice could easily become uncontrollable and simply inundate the claim of tradition. This fear in turn arose from his own full awareness that all political tradition is interlaced with violence and injustice. This is nowhere more boldly admitted than in his "Letter to a Noble Lord" in 1796. This essay was a public response to the Duke of Bedford's attack on the small pension Burke had received upon retirement. The Duke suggested that this award had the taint of corruption. In some of the most biting and precise prose he ever employed, Burke defended himself with an array of arguments. The most arresting of these is his turning of the tables on the Duke. Let us examine, Burke suggests, the terms under which the house of Bedford was established in the sixteenth century. Its founding was accompanied by blood and injustice, as Henry VIII eliminated opponents and rewarded supporters such as the Duke's ancestors.[11] The broad, unstated moral of Burke's assault on the aristocracy is that the very foundation stones of the august, "ancient constitution" of England cover deeply unsettling realities.

There is no clearer indication anywhere in Burke's work of his understanding that contingency in politics goes "all the way down." But the admission here is an exception; he remained convinced that such an insight was generally too dangerous for public expression. We must repress painful knowledge about traditions; "canonization" of forefathers must displace feelings of ambivalence. Burke's rationale for this willful forgetting seems rooted in his fear that such ambivalence is too explosive to be admitted into the politics of the present. "Old violence" must simply be veiled with legitimacy.[12] The ethos of fighting against injustice is now rudely shoved into the background in the name of defending tradition. Moreover, what at first appeared as a reasonable ethos of defending tradition is at this point contaminated once again by what is essentially another version of official theater.

The upshot of the foregoing train of thought is that one cannot cash out Burke's wisdom in any straightforward fashion. All attempts to unearth such wisdom, as in the defense of tradition or the fight against injustice, will have to break radically with the historical Burke at some point. If this is so, then perhaps my attempt to refigure Burke's thinking on the sublime might be regarded with less skepticism than would otherwise be the case.

I can pick up the thread of my idea of an ethos of the sublime at precisely the point where the other two interpretations encountered their difficulties: the repression of the memory of old violence. Burke's adamant commitment to this policy radically displaces a deep source of painfulness in political reflection. However much he may have felt such a policy to be justified as a way of shutting off additional sources of revolutionary motivation, the fact remains that this radical displacement of pain carries with it a deep irony. In a specific sense, it amounts to a kind of curious mimicry of the thrust of revolutionary consciousness. The latter conceived of a future cleansed of contingency and ambivalence; its task for the present was to begin the process of sanitation. Burke is at his best when he exposes how such thinking in effect obliterates the substance of politics. Politics is in essence a sphere of contingency, of "the wholly new and unlooked for."[13] To think that this can be cleaned up in some final sense is precisely the madness he attributes to Jacobinism. But if this is so, is Burke not doing something similar in regard to the *past?* Its contingency is ironed out by the gesture of canonization. Such willful forgetting of contingency in the past constitutes a displacement of just the sort of pain that Burke affirms as being at the core of the authentic sublime.

Burke feared remembrance of pain and injustice because he thought it would be used as a pretext for political revenge.[14] The memory of "old violence" would only foster new violence. This is no doubt a perennial danger to which anyone in politics must be acutely sensitive. We have only to look at the new violence that has emerged in the 1990s out of old ethnic and national hatreds in the former Yugoslavia and the Soviet Union to see what Burke fears. But perhaps we can admit this danger, and yet still not embrace Burke's remedy of repression of memory. Ironically, one might argue that his remedy was precisely the sort of policy pursued by the former authoritarian communist regimes in the areas just mentioned. In short, the admission that Burke has seen a legitimate danger does not yet validate his remedy.

We might consider instead whether a heightened sense of contingency in regard to our *past*—its pain and injustice—might actually aid the cultivation of just the sense of the sublime that Burke wants to see in the *present*. Something of this sense does in fact come through when he employs the image of the aged, infirm parent rather than that of the canonized forefather. The former mirrors our finitude; the latter is a "marvel" of our own creation.

The idea of an individual cultivation of the sublime now begins to take the shape of an ethos that is open to the presence of radical contingency in all spheres of life, past, present, and future. Openness here means an active embracing of contingency as the mirror of human finitude. And this means that we no longer envision what disrupts or dislocates our plans and projects as merely obstacle, but also as reminder. We cultivate the pain of the sublime in everyday life experiences of disjuncture and frustration.[15]

At this point the objection might be raised that a cultivation of the sublime in the midst of the mundane would gut the experience as traditionally understood. The most striking examples of the sublime have typically been associated with things grand, vast, overpowering; in short, things that stand for or evoke the infinite. For example, in the instance I referred to from Burke's early life, the growing threat of a disastrous flood induced reflections on mortality and God. The space for the "delight" of the sublime results from the threat not being immediate; and the source of the delight comes from the contact with what is beyond limits, transcendent, infinite. Although it has thus been typical to represent or evoke the infinite by what is grand or overpowering, it is nevertheless interesting to consider some ways in which this association has been loosened for modern consciousness. Many things that in the eighteenth century still were quite naturally associated with the sublime appear today in a rather different light. A wild animal such as a lion—the symbol of royal power—is less likely to evoke a traditional sense of the sublime in us than a sense of the fragility of a part of nature threatened with extinction. A similar point could be made about oak trees, which were such a potent image for Burke.[16] What this suggests is that nature's "natural" role as supplier of grand moments of sublimity has been radically undermined in the modern world. This role of nature is indeed one of the casualties of the modern spirit of limitless striving. Magnitude and power displays have increasingly shifted to the domain of human production, the human infinite.

If this is so, and if we think that the spirit of Burke's thought would urge us to resist the false sublime, then the cultivation of a sublime of everyday life may no longer seem so inapt. It must be emphasized that this way of vivifying finitude may be connected with different conceptualizations of infinitude. The infinite may be God in a traditional sense, as it was for Burke. It is hardly foreign to Christianity, for example, to connect the being of God with the smallest of objects or occurrences. But the infinite need not be so closely tied to traditional theocentrism. It might just as easily be tied to something like the sheer "presencing" of being that so occupied Heidegger in his later work.[17] However the infinite or "beyond human" is construed, the point of this way of refiguring the sublime is to relocate the experience of finite/infinite at junctures that more effectively put into question the urge to limitlessness embedded in the modern spirit.

Such an ethos would not, as I have said, provide any explicit political principles. It certainly does not justify the inequalities and limitations on individual freedom that Burke endorsed. Our principles can only come from rational reflection upon the affirmative heritage of political modernity: a strong commitment to equality and freedom for all citizens. The ethos of a sublime of everyday life might, however, provide us with a bearing and a humility, in the context of which such reflection and the political action it warrants might be better sensitized to their potential both for engendering injustice and thoughtlessly obliterating tradition.

Notes

1. See Martin Heidegger, *Basic Writings,* ed. D. Krell (New York: Harper & Row, 1977); and *The Question Concerning Technology and Other Essays,* trans. with introduction by W. Lovitt (New York: Harper & Row, 1977). Also Max Horkheimer and Theodor Adorno, *Dialectic of Enlightenment,* trans. J. Cumming (New York: Seabury, 1972). One associates nineteenth- and twentieth-century critiques of modernity not just with complaints about political life, but also with economic life, in particular the imperatives of capitalism and bureaucratic socialism. Although Burke's insights did not really tap into this problem in its broadest sense, some of his remarks about what he saw as the disastrous economic dynamism of the revolutionary system in France are not unrelated to this question. Cf. J.G.A. Pocock, "The Political Economy of Burke's Analysis of the French Revolution," in *Virtue, Commerce, and History* (Cambridge: Cambridge University Press, 1985), pp. 193-212.

2. One especially relevant difference here in some postmodern philosophers is their association of the sublime with what is shocking. Following the notion of the avant-garde earlier in this century, the sublime is humanized and employed as an instrument with which to shock an audience into greater political awareness. From Burke's point of view this would tend too much toward the false sublime. Cf. my discussion of Jacques Derrida in *Political Theory and Postmodernism* (New York: Cambridge University Press, 1991), pp. 75-84.

3. *Reflections, WS,* VIII, p. 85.

4. Friedrich Nietzsche, *Thus Spake Zarathustra,* trans. with introduction by R. J. Hollingdale (Hammondsworth, U.K.: Penguin, 1961), p. 68.

5. "Letter to the National Assembly," *WS,* VIII, p. 332.

6. *Reflections, WS,* VIII, pp. 110-11.

7. See also his remark, noted earlier, about constitutional change being permissible if a "decided majority" favored it; Chapter 1, p. 14.

8. *Inquiry, Works,* I, p. 113.

9. From the impeachment trial, quoted in Paul Hindson and Tim Gray, *Burke's Dramatic Theory of Politics* (Aldershot, U.K.: Avebury, 1988), p. 72.

10. Conor Cruise O'Brien, *The Great Melody: A Thematic Biography* (Chicago: University of Chicago Press, 1992), pp. xxi-xxix, 114-15, 507.

11. "Letter to a Noble Lord," *WS,* IX, pp. 162-70.

12. *Corr.,* VI, p. 95. Burke's doctrine of "presumption" has the primary purpose of blocking the exposure of any ambivalence in tradition.

13. "Remarks on the Policy of the Allies," *WS,* VIII, p. 498.

14. Cf. Bruce James Smith, *Politics and Remembrance* (Princeton, NJ: Princeton University Press, 1985), Chap. 3.

15. Cf. my *Political Theory and Postmodernism,* especially pp. 85-94. My sense is that Jean-François Lyotard has something similar in mind, although the issues are clouded by his implausible theory of language; Lyotard, *The Differend: Phrases in Dispute,* trans. G. Van Den Abbeele (Minneapolis: University of Minnesota Press, 1988).

16. In his unpublished history of England, Burke traced the sense of reverence associated with the oak tree back to the Druids, whose very name, he said, derived from their word for "oak"; "An Essay Towards an Abridgement of the English History," *Works,* VII, p. 183.

17. Cf. my reading of Heidegger in *Political Theory and Postmodernism,* Chap. 4, pp. 85-94.

Index

About the Author

Stephen K. White is Professor of Political Science at Virginia Polytechnic Institute and State University. His publications include *Political Theory and Postmodernism* and *The Recent Work of Jürgen Habermas*. He is also the editor of *Life-World and Politics* and *The Cambridge Companion to Habermas*.